THE SEVEN VIRTUES

THE SEVEN VIRTUES

AN INTRODUCTION TO CATHOLIC LIFE

JEAN DONOVAN

A Herder & Herder Book
The Crossroad Publishing Company
New York

The Crossroad Publishing Company
16 Penn Plaza–481 Eighth Avenue, Suite 1550
New York, NY 10001

Printed in the United States of America on acid-free paper

The text of this book is set in 10.5/13 Stone Informal.
The display faces are Diotima and Stone Informal.

Library of Congress Cataloging-in-Publication Data

Donovan, Jean.
    The Seven virtues : an introduction to Catholic life / Jean
Donovan.
        p.   cm.
    "A Herder & Herder book."
    Includes bibliographical references and index.
    ISBN-13: 978-0-8245-2452-4 (alk. paper)
    ISBN-10: 0-8245-2452-7 (alk. paper)
    1. Cardinal virtues. 2. Catholic Church–Doctrines. 3. Christian
life–Catholic authors.   I. Title.

BV4645.D66 2007
241′.4–dc22   2007000714

1   2   3   4   5   6   7   8   9   10   12   11   10   09   08   07

CONTENTS

Part One
THE THEOLOGICAL VIRTUES

Part Two
THE NATURAL VIRTUES

Part Three
CHOOSING LIFE IN COMMUNITY

INTRODUCTION

Christianity begins with an experience of God. That experience is as alive today as it was back in the days of the early followers who encountered Jesus. Catholic belief and practice begin with the self-gift of God, who calls us into relationship. Theology serves to tell the story of our encounter with God and what it has come to mean to the Christian community over the course of two thousand years. This book on Catholicism remains focused on the lived reality of people, what they have experienced and what they have come to believe about themselves and their relationship to God. For the reader, this book on Catholic belief and practice poses the challenge to take seriously the call to live life intentionally. We begin by laying down a foundation for theology as one would lay the foundation of a house.

The Immensity of Life

It's the immensity of life that gets people thinking about God. And it's our extraordinary ability to sense that immensity that makes such thinking possible. Life is bigger than we are. The stars in the sky draw our eyes upward and outward into the distance of space. The earth revolves from sunlight into darkness, day in and day out, over a seemingly endless expanse of time. Crocuses and tulips push through the snow to herald the coming of spring. A woman labors, and a new human being is pushed into the world. Our own minds, in idle boredom, transport us to the beaches of the Caribbean or to childhood memories of Christmas morning. We live in the present, remember the past, and dream of the future. Even when we succumb to pain, loss, and loneliness, there is something in our human spirit that remains unquenchable.

The language of theology terms this immensity "mystery." Not the mystery of a novel, where one follows the twists and turns the author constructs to solve the case. Rather, it is a fathomless depth that reaches beyond human comprehension or control. In the drama of life — or, better, the drama of the fullness of reality—the human person is sometimes the audience, sometimes the author, sometimes the stage, sometimes the unwitting accomplice. And sometimes, the grandeur and magnitude of the mystery unfolds completely beyond human awareness. The immensity of the mystery is larger than human life, and, according to theology, it always will be.

Wrestling with our finite human existence, its raw beginning and slow disintegration, human beings strive nonetheless to claim and conquer the world laid out before us. We see, feel, hear, smell, and taste the stimuli of our senses. We calculate the passage of time. We live. We take each day, each rock, each tool, each word or idea, and we build a human community. We record our history, teach our children, fly our planes, and chart our course into tomorrow. We question and probe to see what is behind the curtain, what is the cause that invoked our very existence. Why are we alive?

Called to a New Land

Remember the riddle, "Which came first, the chicken or the egg?" We might ask, "Which came first, the human question or the divine call"?[1] For the whole story of Christianity is about encountering God in ordinary life. God comes to us. In the early narratives of the Hebrew Scriptures (later incorporated into the Christian Bible), "The Lord said to Abram: 'Go forth from the land of your kinsfolk and from your father's house to a land that I will show you'" (Genesis 12:1). And so Abraham is called by God to leave the city of Ur in the Tigris-Euphrates river valley and migrate to the land of Canaan. We come to know anything about God because of an encounter. The foundational principle poses its own problems. What role does faith play in this encounter? And as we enter the twenty-first century with the rampant growth of both secularization and antipathy to religious faith, what sense can we make of claims that God has opened the conversation with humanity? Are we discounting the brutal philosophical debates about the possibility of proving the existence of God?

Life is bigger than we are, and yet we find our place in it. Faith provides a fundamental orientation, a way of looking at the world and living our fragile human lives. Thus begins the journey of exploration. Inspired by faith, what choices should we make? Which turns should we take? To what land will we be called?

Being a Christian

In the early centuries of the Christian community, intel-
lectuals, mystics, religious leaders, and faithful followers
began to craft statements of belief. "We believe in one
God...." Jesus' friends, his followers, and his disciples
preached the "good news" that God has come to heal
and save the human race from suffering and death. The
message of love, hope, and faith preached by these first
Christians attracted followers. And so the story of Christianity was told, and the life of Christian prayer was
crafted. To be in relation to God, Christians prayed as
Jesus had instructed them to pray, and gathered together
to break bread and bless wine and say the prayers that
consecrated them into Christ. Faith in Jesus meant a commitment to being a follower, a "disciple," one who would
continue the mission of Jesus, to bring life and healing
to a broken world. The writings of the saints and doctors
of the church, the teachings of the bishops' councils, the
celebrations of the Sunday liturgical gatherings, all con-
tributed to a substantive understanding of what that life of
faith would mean. Each generation made its mark on the
Christian story, and so we come to our own times. What
does this new century offer to the practice and belief of
modern-day Christians?

In the complex world of Christianity today, with the
many traditions, emphases, and priorities among the
Christian churches, it makes sense to talk specifically about
a particular expression of Christianity. In this text we
will focus on the Catholic tradition in the West and its
understanding and practice of the Christian faith. Of

course, all the Christian churches share a common beginning, although the East and West maintained distinct liturgical and theological emphases. Conflicts over the Holy Land led to a severance of ties between the East and West in the eleventh century, and Martin Luther's challenge to the selling of indulgences in the sixteenth century began a series of divisions in the West. The diversity of Christian expressions has only heightened in modern times. The expansion of Christianity in the United States in the eighteenth and nineteenth centuries furthered the differentiation of prayer, belief, and religious practice. There is great value in exploring the differences and richness of Christian expression today. Nonetheless, our goals for this project will focus on how Catholics today express their faith in Jesus and respond to the call of discipleship.

Constructing a Life

In terms of writing a book, which door opens Catholic theology to the reader? "How to" questions seem of most value. Studying theology need not be merely an exercise in understanding complex ideas and theories. Rather, by its nature, it's intended to be a blueprint for living. Theology serves the human community by exploring matters that are of vital interest and have a direct and immediate impact on daily life.

The organizing structure of this text has evolved around the notion of *virtue.* Let me give an example of how virtue inspires, and then I will present its theological and philosophical foundation. One day, in the middle of writing my dissertation, I went to see an old friend of mine in Chicago. I had finished all of my coursework, had my outline accepted by the dissertation committee, and now was facing the daunting task of researching and writing the long and complicated text that would open the final door to my receiving a doctorate. The end seemed a million miles away. Ken O'Malley, a Passionist priest, had been my academic advisor during the years I had studied at Catholic Theological Union. He had become a good friend. That day I was sitting in his office in the library, talking with him about all that was to come, and he said to me, "Writing a dissertation is a test of character." At the time, I didn't fully understand what he was trying to tell me, but in the years that followed, as I struggled with this task, I recognized he was right.

Writing a dissertation is not only about how good your research skills are, or how clever your writing, or how vast your knowledge; it is ultimately about whether you can persist through seemingly endless setbacks, problems, confusion, and delays. It is truly about never giving up, never allowing any particular problem to defeat you. Writing a dissertation was about one's character. I had one reader who used so much red ink on my chapters that they looked like they were bleeding from buckshot wounds. Nothing I wrote seemed satisfactory. I lost books, my research trails went in circles, I spent hours and hours alone sitting in front of a computer, one of my readers resigned, my mother was very ill—the world in which I lived whirled around me in chaos. Trouble dogged me to the end; even the finished text printed on official Fordham dissertation paper had to be completely reprinted because the margins were one-quarter inch too wide.

I remember preparing for the defense. I flew into New York the day before and spent the evening alone in an empty dormitory, reading and rereading my notes. I faced the committee and readers, answered questions and defended decisions I had made at critical junctures in my research. And when all was said and done, they called me doctor. It had been a test of my character, my ability to overcome obstacles, make decisions, endure hardships, and persevere. I felt pure joy and exhilaration, and I felt strong. The dissertation had affected me as a person. Somehow I was different. I had changed.

The Virtuous Life

This experience came to mind when I began to frame the structure for this book on Catholic theology. Theology is not so much what we know or think; it's a way to describe who we are and why we live the way we do. Being faithful to the gospel, taking Christianity seriously and trying to make your life conform to it, is a test of character. It's a life of self-definition and self-discipline. It is difficult, challenging, comforting, and inspiring. A classic way to describe this kind of self-transformation is to talk about virtue. Perhaps there is a certain cultural dissonance when we first think of the idea of virtue. Western culture as we begin a new century is dominated by fast and easy pleasure—by ready access to alcohol and drugs, by consumerism where happiness is a fast car and a big sound system, by the enticement of lottery tickets where the best avenue to wealth and security is to pick six numbers, by the flashing images of television entertainment where excitement, beauty, and success can be experienced vicariously, numbing us to the inadequacies of the life that begins again once the television is turned off. A virtuous life may seem archaic in a world that spouts easy solutions. However, I am going to suggest that the path of true happiness is paved with struggle and suffering, with hard work and self-sacrifice. This is the path of Christian discipleship.

So we are going to take a gamble of a different sort and suggest organizing the chapters of this text around the virtues identified by the Greek philosopher Aristotle (384– 322 BC) and St. Thomas Aquinas, a Dominican monk who lived in the thirteenth century. St. Thomas found inspiration in the rediscovered writings of Aristotle and allowed this philosopher's philosophy to influence his own theology. The seven virtues embraced by St. Thomas — faith, hope, love, prudence, justice, temperance, and fortitude— will provide a window into the soul of Christianity. When Aristotle wrote about virtue in his *Nicomachean Ethics,* it seems to me that his mind was focused on the characteristics of a man, and, in particular, a man who goes into battle. What kind of a man is willing to risk his life? And why does he do so? This question is central to the way Aristotle defines virtue. For according to Aristotle, virtue is not one's passions or one's faculties; rather it is a "state of character."[2]

Aristotle reflects on the habit of courage, right actions for the right reasons that do not fall to excess. The virtue of courage comprises voluntary actions exercised within a range of behaviors, not falling into excess by foolhardiness or falling short through cowardice. A courageous man loves his life, but carefully risks it for a greater good. What seems to impress Aristotle the most is that the virtuous man's motives match his actions. There is no self-serving interest that secretly inspires an apparently good action. No, the action reveals the goodness within it. Virtue is a way of life. It comes alive for all to see as the actual actions take place. I don't think Aristotle would be satisfied with right belief or values if they did not have an impact on one's actions. Rather, he sees the virtues embodied through repeated exercise.

The Lens of Virtue

Aristotle identified many topics in the course of his argument defining virtue: courage, temperance, liberality, magnificence in matters of money, pride, ambition, honor, good temper, friendliness, truthfulness, ready wit in social intercourse, shame, and justice. Even friendship can be seen through the lens of virtue, for it is based on the free gift of care and concern for the other, without attention to the personal profit that might be achieved through the relationship. When St. Thomas Aquinas outlines his understanding of virtue in the *Summa Theologica,* he revisits Aristotle's fundamental principles about the nature of virtue, but agrees with St. Ambrose's list of four: temperance, justice, prudence, and fortitude.[3] With these four virtues of human behavior, he also points to three "theological" virtues, which God inspires in us: faith, hope, and love. His perspective on these virtues is rooted in the letters of St. Paul in the New Testament. In particular, when Paul is writing to the Corinthians, he explains the gifts each person gives and receives within the Christian community. And he addresses the power of love in chapter 13:

> If I speak in human and angelic tongues but do not have love, I am a resounding gong of a clashing cymbal. And if I have the gift of prophecy and comprehend all mysteries and all knowledge; if I have all faith so as to move mountains, but do not have love, I am nothing. If I give away everything I own, and if I hand my body over so that I may boast but do not have love, I gain nothing. . . . At present we see indistinctly, as in a mirror, but then face to face. At present I know partially; then I shall know fully, as I am fully known. So faith, hope, love remain, these three; but the greatest of these is love. (1 Corinthians 13:1–3; 12–13)

For Thomas, faith, hope, and love are supernatural virtues because they open the door for us to inherit the promise of eternal life, made possible through God's creative act: "Let us make man in our image, after our likeness" (Genesis 1:26). Faith, hope, and love are ultimately human experiences that unite us to God.

Granted, our worldview might not be the same as that of St. Thomas, and we might not make the same divisions between natural and supernatural virtues. Nonetheless, turning toward the notion of virtue opens up a path through mountains of theology and history. We can see the simple meaning in virtue: a life built on choices that transform a person into someone admirable, someone deserving of respect, someone trustworthy. And if we can connect that human experience with the profound meanings of the depth of the spiritual nature of the human person, where we find a longing for more — more love, more freedom, more life — then we are on our way toward touching the heart of the Christian faith.

The Christian Story

Our starting point has been the immensity of life that surrounds us and the way in which the human person finds a way to construct a life within it. Included in this perspective is the way that theology is rooted in the Christian story. It's life in the particular, in the here and now, theology in a context. As we stand at the beginning of the twenty-first century, we look back on two thousand years of Christian history. Christians today share a common story with those who have gone before them. That story is remembered by the first followers of Jesus, recorded in bits and pieces that become the collection of sacred writings called the New Testament. The writings of the New Testament are bound together with the ancient laws and customs of the people of Israel, their prayer and wisdom, their history and experience of God. In the New Testament eyewitness accounts that tell of Jesus' life and teaching are recorded in the Gospels. They describe the way he healed the sick and suffering, encouraged those who listened with his teachings, called them to a greater love of God and neighbor, and died and miraculously returned to them.

The struggles of the early church are recorded, and some of the letters of Paul, Peter, and other church leaders are preserved. The narratives include a prophecy of the coming of the Spirit, who would guide the church into the future. And they describe how the community experienced that Spirit. Over the centuries, the church built on this foundation. It continued to experience that Spirit and be inspired by the Gospels. Saints and healers, preachers, writers, leaders, individually and communally bound, many followers tell the Christian story, live a life of discipleship. Their story is recorded in the history of the church, in the teachings of the councils, in the theological writings preserved over the centuries. This Christian story continues to be lived out today.

The Mystery of Everyday Life

Some books try to prove the truth of the Christian story. And although the issue of faith, one of the virtues, will be addressed, this text is not designed to convince anyone to conform to Christian life by an intellectual argument. For as John Henry Newman wrote in the nineteenth century, "A man convinced against his will, is of the same opinion still." Neither coercive nor persuasive, this book is more like "show and tell." Here is the Christian story, and watch how people take up their cross and follow Jesus. But on the other hand, who reads a text without an expectation that something useful will come of the effort? So each chapter invites the reader to explore the possibilities inherent in each virtue.

Our foundation has been laid. We experience the openness of our horizons, the endless possibilities and limited actualities, the distance of the stars and the depths of the seas. Within this world of wonder, we find ourselves and make a life. Although fully alive as sensate animals, we find ourselves longing for eternity. This leads us to reflect on the meaning of our lives, and the purpose of life itself draws us into the mystery that is the stuff of theological reflection. One way to unpack the complex writings and thought patterns of theology is to consider them in relation to ordinary life. What impact does theology have on what people say and do every day? This leads us to a potential wealth of insight by considering the classic concept of virtue. And so this text will consider theology by examining faith, hope, love, prudence, justice, temperance, and fortitude, not simply as the way for the warrior of fourth-century BC Athens, but as expressed in the lives of Christians whose experience of God in the person of Jesus Christ has been etched into the course of human history. Our last foundation block broadens our scope to see the way this individual course of discipleship exists in relation to both mystery and community.

Religious Experience

There are many ways to explore the experience of mystery. In our case, we see it through the lens of the Christian story. But that story does not stand outside of human history. Our one world is shared by all, from one age to another. Joachim Wach (1898–1955) was a scholar of comparative religion, perhaps because his own life was a bridge between different worlds. He was born in Germany and taught at the University of Leipzig during the rise of Nazism. His ancestors were Jewish, although he was a devout Anglican, and his family suffered at the hands of the

Nazis. He spent the war years in the United States. He went to India near the end of his life to give a series of lectures, and there he hoped to share a vocabulary and a method for talking about religious experience that could be universal. His lectures were published after his death as *The Comparative Study of Religions.*[4] According to Wach, genuine religious experience is expressed in thought, action, and fellowship (that is, community).

Wach's instinct that human beings are spiritual and that across cultures, religions, and traditions we can find common threads makes sense to me. His thinking has inspired the structure of this text, as well as its goals. For as much as we want to say what the Christian story means, we can and should do so within the larger context of the world community. Time and again we discover how much we share in common and how grim are the consequences of dividing people one against the other. Wach was able to find hope and unity at the end of his life, after much suffering caused by racial, ethnic, and religious hatred. In harmony with Wach's instinct that the notion of genuine religious experience creates common ground, we will explore the ways in which the Christian story finds fellow travelers.

From Part One on theological virtues, through Part Two on natural virtues, our text moves to Part Three on communion. Religious experience expressed in action and community, as Wach would term it, allows us to explore the way in which human beings relate to God and to one another. The Christian life is not conceived ultimately as an isolated, independent journey. The virtuous life is not mere spiritual athleticism. It's a life shared with others, in response to an experience of the presence of God. In Part Three we will look at the rituals that express that response. And finally, we will look again at the challenges life poses and the way in which Catholic doctrine expresses a community's answer.

Part One

The Theological Virtues

Chapter One

FAITH

So faith, hope, love remain, these three: but the greatest of these is love.   —1 Corinthians 13:13

◆ ◆ ◆

CHRISTIANS MUST LIVE a life of faith. But what does that mean? What is faith? This is our first question. As we began this inquiry, we touched on the concept of mystery, the infinity of the universe, the intricacies of human existence, the intensity of our dreams and longings. Life is a powerful force, drawing us in and sweeping us along. We can just be swept along, from day to day, meal to meal, until one day we die. Or we can live life intentionally, finding purpose and meaning in what we do, why we do it, where we are going, and how we are going to get there. Living every day provokes questions of meaning and purpose, questions of faith. Once you begin to wonder, it's easy to see how much faith is taken for granted in everyday life.

On every level of ordinary life, we find ourselves in a place where we must choose to have faith in others. Is the aspirin in the bottle properly made? Is the lettuce in your

salad clean and safe to eat? Did your doctor pay attention and work hard in medical school? Will that person
actually stop at the red light? If I have a heart attack,
will you give me CPR? Human existence is a life lived in a
web of connections, interlocking mechanisms of shared responsibilities. We need each other, and in our dependence
we learn to trust each other. But faith encompasses much
more. We have faith in each other; we learn to have faith
in ourselves. We struggle through our youth to become a
person, with an identity, personality traits, skills, interests,
abilities. Experience teaches us about ourselves. And we
may come to a happy point some day with confidence in
ourselves, in the way we live our lives. But faith still lies
deeper.

MARIA HUDDLES with her five children behind a garbage
dumpster, in the back of a gasoline station, one block away
from the apartment where she lives, waiting for the friend
she called to pick them up. She's carrying with her a few
duffel bags filled with clothes and toys. She had these
packed for days, hidden under the dirty laundry. After her
husband left for work that morning, she kicked into gear a
plan of escape that she had mentally rehearsed over and
over again. She quickly dressed her children, running to
the window every few minutes to check and make sure
that he had not turned around to come home. Her heart
was pounding as they crossed the street, heading to the
gas station. There she was able to call her friend Janet.
As planned, Maria and her children then hid behind the
dumpster where Janet was to meet them. While waiting,
Maria began to tremble. She knew that her husband could

decide to leave work and come home, sensing that she was trying to leave him. Returning to the empty apartment, he would search for them. And he would find them. The consequences would be severe. He would drag her back, screaming and yelling at her, and then beat her once he had her back in the apartment. The kids would run and hide in the closet, witnesses to a familiar ordeal.

AND YET, SHE WAS THERE, waiting and hoping. She was in fact moving forward, propelled by something. She did not know if she would be safe; she did not know if she would succeed. All she knew was the power her husband had over her, and the pain he would cause her. Yet she dove into the darkness of the unknown, risking everything.[1]

I met Maria in a shelter for battered women. Her story echoes the lives of many people who find the ability to believe in goodness, in an unknown power in their lives that helps them to reach out for that goodness, no matter what the risk. Faith is like an underground current flowing through one's life, mind, and body. And religious faith calls that current the presence of God in one's life.

We begin our explorations into the nature of a Christian life by considering first the three theological virtues: faith, hope, and love. Christians find inspiration from the writings of St. Paul, who talked about these virtues to the people in the churches around the Mediterranean, where he traveled and preached the good news. We will consider a Catholic theologian's understanding of faith, as it is expressed in connection with ultimate reality. Roger Aubert, a priest and professor of church history at the University of Louvain, centers his definition of faith on the fundamental principle that faith is a supernatural act.[2] It is a gift from God, a choice, freely made, and it is rational. It does not violate the wealth of knowledge and scientific acumen that we have achieved as a human community. We will address the relationship between faith and reason, and the spiritual angst created by unanswered prayers. Being faithful to one's belief in God and the ultimate meaningfulness of life also calls for a commitment to be faithful to oneself and to others. All of these dimensions of the challenge of faith need to be considered.

Theological Foundations

Faith is a response, an answer to a call. The starting point in theological reflection on faith is the idea of *revelation*. We come to know anything about God, because God initiates communication. Faith is built on a relationship, not on an intellectual theory. At the heart of the Christian story is the experience of a group of people who came into contact with a man named Jesus. Their experiences and beliefs are expressed in the writings of the New Testament, and those experiences were filtered through the lens of first-century Israel and the religious and cultural roots of Judaism. To grasp the essence of Christian faith, Catholics return again and again to read, to think, to pray, and to celebrate this rich tradition. The book of Acts in the New Testament describes the transition period, how Jesus appeared after his resurrection and guided the early church until his ascension. And then the Spirit of God descends on the community at Pentecost, to stay with them and guide them. The faith of the early Christians was inspired by a sense of the closeness of God's Spirit.

What guides Christians today? Where is that closeness of God in ordinary life, two thousand years after those first followers? For that is the challenge we face, to find our own experience of the presence of God. The Catholic Church has always trusted that the Spirit continued to guide the Christian community, that the experience of the later generations was as valid as that of the early church. So one should expect in our own times to find God. An American Catholic theologian, Lawrence Cunningham, writes in a text on Catholicism of the ways in which we come to know God today.[3] Let us consider some ways in which God's presence is revealed to us.

Amazing Nature

Imagine a sunset, streams of gold, orange, and red across a still-bright sky. Look over your shoulder, and the sky is dark. Look back again, and it is light. Imagine climbing to the top of a mountain ridge. The peaks were formed ages ago, as the earth beneath was formed, and changed, and reformed. Even the trees around you have lived longer than you. You are in the ocean, swimming in crystal-blue clear water, watching the fish all around you. You flip in the waters, and float on your back. You look up into the heavens; the clouds are soft balls of fluff.

Smell the newly cut grass in your backyard in the summertime. Pull an apple off the tree and eat it. Whether it is the smell of salt water and the pounding of the waves on the Atlantic, the buzz of mosquitoes deep in the woods, or the crunch of snow underfoot on the way to the ski lodge, nature is amazing. The natural world astounds us with its beauty, its order, its complexity, and its life. The world has a life of its own, and seems to carry on around us, quite indifferent to human beings. And when it roars? Lightning flashes, thunder booms, rain pours down. The earth rumbles, shakes, and cracks. Frigid winds blast, snow flies and piles up between us and anywhere we want to go. Ignore that roar at your own peril.

Nature draws us into considering the immensity of life. The endless sky and burning stars show how small our planet is in the cosmos. Staring up into the night sky sometimes dwarfs us, but in other ways may be a comfort. We are part of a universe, a small part at that. But when religious people talk about an infinite creator God, the world affirms that possibility more than it disallows it. The natural world allows us to imagine something infinitely bigger than we are.

The Unfolding of History

The unfolding of history, as Cunningham states, draws us back into human life, craft, discovery, and productivity. Studying our own progress through time and space, the development of cultures and technologies, the bravery and inventiveness of our forefathers and foremothers opens another avenue for finding the presence of God. Human history is chronicled in the writings of historians, in the buildings and inventions that surround us, in the medicine we take to stop an infection, in the jets we fly from coast to coast. "What a piece of work is a man, how noble in reason, how infinite in faculties, in form and moving, how express and admirable," wrote the Shakespeare. "How infinite in faculties," how amazing the accomplishments of human beings. In our own times, we have seen advances in science and medicine, in public consciousness over domestic violence and abuse, the breaking down of the Berlin Wall. The growth of the principles of democracy and freedom in the West has made an impact on world history. The harsh realities of violence, terrorism, and war that marked the beginning of the twenty-first century should make us pause. And in fact the reality of human destructive hatred might end an innocent trust in the goodness of life, and raise the question of where God's presence lies when people kill each other. But without rushing to simplistic statements about God, it is still possible to see the goodness and light that shine within the course of human history.

Institutions

The social reality of institutions marks the way memory is embedded in cultures. In the United States the growth of and support for public schools is a prime example. Legislation and customs support the right of every child born in the United States to access the knowledge of human society, to develop his or her potential, and to participate in the common life of the community. Hospitals, homeless shelters, centers for grieving children, domestic violence centers, hospice care for the dying, police departments, ambulance corps, and fire departments are populated with everyday heroes. Society celebrates Little League players and ballerinas, baked cakes and prize pumpkins, the big and small surprises and delights in life. Even the silly traditions of Santa Claus, a chubby fellow coming down the chimney to give toys to good little girls and boys, reveal a playfulness and generosity inherent in society. In the humming of a Christmas carol, or the purchase of Girl Scout cookies, society brings us reasons to hope, and laugh, and find life meaningful. When life is worthwhile, would it be difficult to see that God intends such value and purpose?

The Goodness and Holiness of Others

When you love someone, doesn't that person seem larger than life? Would it be possible to be so inspired by someone that you would willingly change your life to be with that person? Would you be willing to make whatever sacrifices necessary, to live up to the standards they set, to live as they lived? Our lives are intimately connected. We are a human family, a community bound through shared struggles, dreams, and hopes. Your story is the story of the human race. Cunningham says that the goodness and holiness of others reveal God's presence to us. Where does that goodness come from? The Christian community recalls the simple wisdom of the Genesis narratives, where God makes the human form and calls humans into life by infusing God's own image and likeness into that form. The Christian community shares a simple faith in the deep inner connection of God and humankind—a sense that a man's life, a woman's life, shares in God's own life force. Our life is God's life, our goodness and holiness are God's goodness and holiness.

Sacramental Life and the Word of God

The overtly religious expressions of the Christian tradition, Cunningham believes, also are able to draw us into the presence of God. The rituals that recall Jesus' words and actions at the last meal he shared with his followers have long been incorporated into the communal worship celebrations. "The Word" that is preached is found in the writings of the New Testament. The Gospels recall the life, ministry, death, and resurrection of Jesus. The letters of Paul and others address problems in the first Christian communities. And of course the Word is richly expressed in the story of salvation history that begins with the faith of the people of Israel, with those ancestors who placed their lives in God's hands, hearing that call and responding as the prophet Isaiah did as a young man, "Here I am, Lord, send me!" When the community gathers together to recall its history of faith in God, it finds that God is with them once again. In particular, the Catholic heritage finds that certain rituals called *sacraments* celebrate life and open the human family to God's presence. These rituals combine the ordinary and the divine, ordinary time and eternity. The sacraments help to focus the transitions of life—birth, adulthood, marriage, old age, and death—so that they take place in sacred time, in God's presence.

Life itself draws us toward recognizing the deeper current running through our lives, that force of life that beckons us onward. It is our life together, marrying and giving birth, donating blood and rescuing people from blazing fires, our stories, our aches and pains, our dreams and ambitions, all of this is where we find God. God is in the night sky and in the sea below. God is in the sun and moon and stars. God is in our books, our stories, plays, and celebrations. When we wonder where God is, and if God is, it is the Catholic tradition's response to say: just look around you.

Building on this understanding of God's presence, we move on to think about the response of faith. It seems that life does not easily answer all questions about meaning and purpose. If it is true that God is present to us in myriad ways, it also is true that we must still turn toward that presence, that rather than being self-evident, God is still grasped through the act of faith. Faith is a choice, not a given. Perhaps we could imagine another kind of world and a different way of belonging in the universe. We certainly could imagine a world without war. But without the power to reconstruct life, we mortals must live within the reality we experience. And that reality does not prove the existence of God. So we must make a decision.

Faith as Supernatural

According to Roger Aubert, the act of faith is supernatural, depends on free will, and falls in line with our ability to reason. Faith is a gift from God. That is to say, our ability to transcend space and time, to imagine immortality, is possible because of the way in which we are made, the way in which we share something of God's nature. *Surnaturel*, beyond or above nature, is a manner of describing the place of faith. Philosophers across time and cultures have wrestled with the notion of "immortality." Plato, of ancient Greece, thought this mortal life was just a passing thing. The image he used was that of a cave, where here on earth we see only shadows of the true, immortal reality that we will experience after we shed this flesh, which burdens and distorts our true selves, our immortal souls.[4]

Perhaps it is true that all religions articulate some vision of life after death; however, they differ in their understandings. Humanity it seems has always imagined and proposed the possibility that this mortal life does not completely contain and control our human nature. Somehow we are more. Christians see that immortality as a gift from God. Why? At creation, God made the human being with a *soul*. We have a spiritual essence that coexists, commingles with our humanness. Of course this is a statement of belief. We believe we have a soul, which is the place where we experience the presence of God, the way in which we are connected to that divine presence.

Faith as a Choice

Faith is an act. It is a choice; it demands commitment. And it is freely made. Human beings act in freedom. The wisdom of sociology, psychology, and philosophy might offer correctives to that statement. It may very well be true that society, our childhood experiences, our ethnic, cultural, and religious heritage frame the way we think, shape our values, the ways that we perceive and define reality. Some currents of the Christian tradition argue for God's hand as more actively directive in our lives. But the Catholic tradition holds to the understanding that human beings have the fundamental power to come to know themselves, pursue the purpose and meaning of their own lives, and find a path to a true faith commitment. The church does recognize the moral struggle in life to find truth, honesty, courage, and faithfulness, and it does acknowledge human sinfulness. Our sinfulness can indeed affect our ability to know God and to live freely. Spiritual direction and pastoral care with the sacrament of reconciliation are ways in which the church responds to the distortions of freedom that influence our lives. But ultimately the human person is capable of acting freely and responding to God's call.

Faith as Rational

Along with this acknowledgment of human freedom comes an understanding that faith in God does not violate human reason. The history of the Catholic Church includes some rather infamous evidence to the contrary. In 1632 Galileo was called before the Inquisition to answer for his scientific theories.[5] As the nineteenth century drew to a close, the First Vatican Council, so often remembered for its teaching on papal infallibility, also taught that reason and faith were compatible.

> Even though faith is above reason, there can never be any real disagreement between faith and reason, since it is the same God who reveals the mysteries and infuses faith, and who has endowed the human mind with the light of reason. God cannot deny himself, nor can truth ever be in the opposition to truth.[6]

And that continues to be true today. In 1998 Pope John Paul II wrote an encyclical entitled *Fides et Ratio* (Faith and reason). He begins by saying that "faith and reason are like two wings on which the human spirit rises to the contemplation of truth."[7] As he discusses the historical connection between theology and philosophy, tracing the ways in which St. Paul and the early church fathers connected their preaching with the intellectual knowledge and patterns of reasoning of the Greco-Roman culture, he points to the teachings of the Second Vatican Council (1963–65), which support the compatibility of faith and reason. He reaffirms this position, noting that all human beings are called to pursue the truth in life:

> All men and women, as I have noted, are in some sense philosophers and have their own philosophical conceptions with which they direct their lives. In one way or other, they shape a comprehensive vision and an answer to the question of life's meaning; and in the light of this they interpret their own life's course and regulate their behavior.[8]

New creative possibilities exist when theology and modern knowledge connect. Catholic theologian John Haught, professor of theology at Georgetown University, proposed a "theology of evolution," in response to Darwin's insights.[9] He pointed to the challenge that Jesuit Pierre Teilhard de Chardin placed before the Christian community to respond to the theories of evolution:

> Toward the end of his life, the famous Jesuit paleontologist Teilhard de Chardin (1881–1955) observed that traditional theological reflection has conceived of

God's influence on nature too much in terms of Aristotle's notion of a prime mover pushing things from the past (*a retro*). Evolution, Teilhard said, requires that we think of God not as driving or determining events from behind or from the past, but as drawing the world from up ahead (*ab ante*) toward the future.[10]

Haught found that task to be worthwhile and took up the challenge.

To summarize the thinking of Roger Aubert: faith is supernatural, it is a choice, and it is rational. Now we turn to see how faith comes alive in the lives of persons who have committed themselves to a Christian life.

Life as a Spiritual Journey

Christians must live a life of faith. What does that mean? To commit oneself to faith is to begin a journey. The decision to live with faith must be made again and again. It is not a decision made in childhood, early adulthood, at the moment of confirmation, at twenty-one years of age, or at any other single moment in life. It is a commitment that must be made every day.

One way to explore the meaning of this kind of commitment is to examine the theory of life stages proposed by Erik Erikson. In his book *Childhood and Society,* Erikson introduced his eight-stage theory of human development. Beginning with infancy, the human being faces social and psychological challenges. Each challenge marks a turning point; as each stage is transversed new struggles emerge.

The first stage is Trust vs. Mistrust, and it occurs in the first year of life.[11] An infant reaches out to the world, completely dependent upon her caregivers. Her life or death is determined by their ability to meet her needs, to feed her and clothe her, keep her dry, warm, and comforted. The care she receives gives her a fundamental lesson about human existence: to trust or not to trust. If her needs are met, then she learns that life is trustworthy. If her needs are not met, then she experiences chaos and uncertainty.

What Erikson showed through his research and writing is the profound consequences of each of the life stages. Through his psychological care of young patients, and his efforts to train psychologists at Harvard and elsewhere, Erikson showed the power of these challenges. And once addressed, the fundamental crisis was not eliminated, only subdued. Erikson's theory seemed to play out in the lives of adopted children from Eastern Europe and Russia who came from orphanages to join American families.

Therapists diagnosed "Reactive Attachment Disorder," which is a failure to bond to others as a result of neglect and isolation that disrupt the healthy development of trust and openness to love. It seems to indicate the severe consequences of "mistrust" resulting from the lack of care in that first year. What is intriguing to me, as I consider Erikson's life crises, is that such deep decisions must be made, even in the most primitive stage of life, that of infancy. In a dialogue with the world around her, the infant assesses the most basic aspects of life and crafts a psychological stance. Is there a bridge to the spiritual life? What if the same holds true for our spiritual life? What if we must make a fundamental decision about the world, and with that decision we create our own inner self? And what if those decisions must be reinvented throughout life? Then what we have discovered is the spiritual life.

Faith is a baby crying. Faith is the fundamental choice that life is worth living, that meaning and purpose and love and care exist. A baby cries because he trusts. He knows it is worth crying, because someone will hear and come to him. Faith is opening yourself up to life and believing in others and in God. And what would challenge that faith? Suffering. Meaninglessness. Rejection. Failure. Heartbreak. Tragedy. There are so many brutal experiences that push us to this fundamental challenge once again: to trust or not to trust. The spiritual life of a Christian does not depend solely on the love and care of others, however important these may be. Ultimately, faith rests on trust in God. We recall the words of one of the prayers of the Old Testament, Psalm 23:

> The Lord is my shepherd; I shall not want.
> In verdant pastures he gives me repose;
> beside restful waters he leads me;
> he refreshes my soul....
> Yea though I walk through the valley of the shadow
>   of death,
> I fear no evil, for thou art with me.

Anyone may choose to hold on to faith, regardless of the circumstances of life. Trust rooted in faith in God can stand firm against the storms of life. Of course, that kind of deep trust is rooted in maturity, rooted in a person who has moved through the stages Erikson identified and come to the fullness of adulthood, rooted in a moral strength and character that refuse to be defeated by the vagaries of life, the sinfulness of others, or the trials and hardships of an existence bound by limits, aging, and mortality.

Who would have that strength to hold on to faith under any circumstances? Christians turn to their brothers and sisters, today and yesterday, to find exemplars of faith. We draw strength from the community in which we live and share our stories to find that courage in each other, to help and support and guide and comfort. Faith is a choice nurtured in community.

Conclusion

As Moses drew near the end of his life, after all that he had done to lead the people of Israel out of Egypt and through the Sinai Desert, he came to understand that he would not live to see the Promised Land. Before he died, he spoke to the people one more time, setting before them a choice of two paths: "I have set before you life and death, the blessing and the curse. Choose life, then, that you and your descendants may live, by loving the Lord, your God, heeding his voice, and holding fast to him. For that will mean life for you" (Deuteronomy 30:19–20). This is a lesson to all who live this mortal life.

We all must choose for ourselves, must find a path of our own. We could imagine an easier life, a world that never provoked us to question and rebel against it. But that imaginary world does not answer the question of what to do with the world we know. What is then the choice that will bring us life? Between trust and mistrust, between

faith and doubt, one must actively, willingly, openly, cre-
atively, purposely choose faith. And that choice must be
lived out every day of our lives. Some days may be easier
than others.

How is faith possible? Through God, who called us
into life and relationship. For faith is supernatural, not a
human skill, but a divine seed. Faith begins when we open
ourselves to God's presence within us, around us. We lean
into a power that is stronger than we are, that sustains us
and this universe. But faith is not emptying ourselves of
our intelligence or free will. The Catholic tradition holds
firm to the belief that faith is the answer to the human
quest for truth, that our best intellectual and rational abilities, and the inherited wisdom of the human race, is the
fertile ground in which faith will grow.

And so we have launched ourselves on this journey, a
search to understand what a Christian life might be. And
in discussing this first virtue, faith, we find that it is eminently human, eminently divine. Faith is a baby crying.
Faith is a journey of the strong. Faith is a virtue, acquired
through careful study, effort, and encouragement by a
community of fellow travelers.

Chapter Two

HOPE

I am going to Jerusalem. What will happen to me there I do not know, except that in one city after another the Holy Spirit has been warning me that imprisonment and hardships await me. Yet, I consider life of no importance to me, if only I may finish my course and the ministry that I received from the Lord Jesus, to bear witness to the gospel of God's grace.

—Acts 20:22–24 (Paul to the presbyters of the church at Ephesus)

◆ ◆ ◆

I F FAITH CONNECTS US to God and to all of life, then hope points to the way we are going to live our lives. Hope projects into the course of human history, and it reflects a willingness to endure the hardships of life for the sake of the good we know and love, and for the sake of what the future holds for us. How do we learn to live with hope? What role does Christian faith play in one's commitment to the future? And what are the dangers involved in this journey toward hope?

43

Theological Foundations

Hope is opening oneself to believing that life is good, that human beings are supposed to be happy. As we talked about the challenges to faith, to trusting in God and in others, we realized there are common threads that bind faith and hope, for both of these virtues involve a life struggle against human suffering. Ordinary life poses many problems. For some, it has been reduced to a struggle for survival — finding food, water, and shelter. For too many of the world's population, that is the case. Even those who have achieved a level of physical comfort and security experience loneliness, isolation, failure, rejection. The world around us — nature, society, community, and family — at times is indifferent, or even hostile. And our own bodies betray us, bringing illness and pain, aging and eventual death. Faith marks a commitment to life, but hope is the energy that keeps us in the struggles of life. Hope's greatest enemy: evil. And its opposite, the force pulling against it, is despair.

The term "evil" has been used to describe the destructive energies embedded in human culture, and even nature itself, with its hurricanes, earthquakes, storms, and floods. At times in Christian history, evil has had a name: Satan. Is there a personification of evil, one who plots against the human race and is its enemy? Is evil a dark force found within the human person, a pull toward envy, hatred, fear of the other? Is evil random or purposeful? Is evil just a misrepresentation of the imperfections of an evolving race and universe? We can't seem to escape these questions. To have a life, to be someone in the world and find your way, you must wrestle with the problem of evil. Suffering and loss provoke the temptation to despair, to conclude that life is not worth living, that there is no meaning or purpose to one's existence, no loving presence in the universe. Evil makes us choose: hope or despair.

Hope is not blind. Hope is not naïve or foolish. Hope is wise and strong, confronting the reality of evil and living in spite of it. Hope calls upon us to marshal our courage, our endurance, and our vision of a world to come, where good has finally conquered evil. The temptation to despair makes this life of hope as a Christian more poignant. When confronted with evil, we are called to respond with hope. That hope is not whistling in the dark; it is connecting with some basic principles of Catholic life and teaching.

Grace emerged from the long story of Christianity as a way to describe the effect of God's presence in the world. God's goodness is not self-contained. Rather it pours forth into all of creation, including human beings. God's creation continues to be sustained by that same life force that called it into being. How do we know that grace exists? Of course, we know by faith. But we also know through experience. For the goodness of God is reflected in the world around us — the beauty of nature, the sounds of a symphony, the pleasure of love, the kindness and generosity of loved ones and strangers. Grace is experienced in the rituals of worship, where a community gathers in prayer to answer God's call. It is not by human effort alone that we find the strength to face evil; rather we are bathed in the goodness of life that comes from God and through that experience of goodness we are empowered. The long story of Christian life is full of intense experiences of the presence of God. The tradition of the mystics, Christians who have found union and joy in divine encounters, shows us the possibilities of encounters with grace.[1]

In the Face of Evil

Fortifying a Christian commitment to hope is the belief in eternal life. Even when life crushes and defeats us, when all the good we do ends in naught, there is more to life than this world. The fundamental reality that Jesus preached is that the Kingdom of God is at hand. Jesus' life and ministry, his death and resurrection, are a sign of the world to come, a sign that it was God's intention when humanity was created for men and women to enjoy communion with God. Endowed with a soul, the human being has a divine destiny. The possibility of immortality has been raised again and again across human history and cultures. For Christians, belief in eternal life was affirmed in the resurrection of Jesus and the promise of the world to come. The Catholic tradition held on to the belief that every human being is accountable for how we live our lives, and that we answer to God at the end of our lives. Heaven and hell mark the opposite ends of human destiny, and the idea of purgatory developed in Catholic thought to explain how it is that an imperfect human could possibly enjoy eternal happiness in communion with God. Trusting in the promise of eternal life offers comfort to those who labor for justice, for human dignity.

Trust in God is possible then, but not easy. Living with hope means fighting against the forces of evil that sometimes overpower and crush us. What pulls against us is the temptation to despair.

Giving Up

Many years ago when I was in college, I heard the news that a young man I knew had killed himself. It was sophomore year, and I was away in France on an exchange program. Some friends and I had received letters from him, chatty, pleasant news from back home. He was living off campus that fall. We were told that he turned the gas on in the oven and put his head into it. The year was 1975.

James Reilly had been in our freshman class. He was slight and had a gentle demeanor. I could remember his blond hair and sweet, somewhat ironic smile. He had invited me on a date to hear Gordon Lightfoot in concert on campus, and I had accepted. He wore a white shirt, with an embroidered sun on the back. The date hadn't gone well for me. I vaguely remember why. I didn't find him attractive, no spark, no excitement. I declined a second date, and he faded away. When I heard the news that he had killed himself, I was stunned. And I relived my own role in his life. How important had that date been to him? Had he cared about me? Did I do something wrong? Could I have prevented what happened? I will never know. But I can't help but wish that he had not reached a point where his despair overrode everything else within him.

As students thirty years ago, we didn't know anything about suicide prevention. We didn't talk about depression or isolation. I think I heard about James's death from another student. I don't remember any official word from the institution, or any meeting or conversation as a group. James died and quietly faded away.

Despair. How is it that a human person collapses under the weight of his or her own suffering? And is this question related to our discussion of hope? Out of respect for James's memory and out of concern for the many young adults who struggle with depression, it's important to raise the issue of suicide. Mental health professionals have researched and written a great deal about suicide in the last thirty years, and they have certainly influenced the way that the church responds to this crisis.

College students experience suicidal thoughts and depression in higher numbers than most people think. Why should they? It's an exciting time of life, away from the rules and controls of home and high school, days filled with building your own dreams. How could this provoke bad feelings? In fact, it does. Young people travel into a "no-man's land" of change. They leave behind the security of home, where they have a place and know that place, into a world of strangers, where they have to prove themselves over and over again, day after day, in the classroom, in the dorm. They must carve out a new place to belong. The competitive nature of academic life heightens the pressures they feel, as does the social circle of dating. James fits the profile of a student at risk,[2] feeling alone in a crowd, feeling that he cannot excel in the university where he has had the privilege to be admitted. He needs to be a star to live up to everyone's expectations, including his own. But in fact, he feels like a failure. These experiences are shared by many young people who must navigate in murky waters to find themselves and make a future. But research shows that it takes a unique combination of circumstances for these feelings to crystallize into a suicide attempt.

Suicide is the narrowing of options into one: to end the pain, the one and only solution is to end one's life. That narrowing is the result of a combination of things all coming together at once. It is the result of acute mental anguish, enflamed by circumstances that are read as impossible to overcome.[3] The world outside crushes suicidal persons, and they follow old habits of quick and impulsive decision making. They can see no other way, even though they might wish they could. Intervention is possible, by opening up options, by limiting the impulsive behaviors, and by rallying the support of those people who play a significant role in their life.[4]

As we think through what the mental health professionals have learned about the suicidal state and strategies for intervention, it seems clear that despair is not ordinarily characterized by suicidal thoughts or feelings. The temptation to suicide seems to be deeply imbedded in psychological and emotional upset and inner worldly struggles confusing the human psyche, and it is treatable with the help of mental health professionals and caring family and friends. Perhaps, then, we characterize despair as the temptation to disengagement with life, to cynicism, laziness, selfishness, and indifference. To despair means to not care, to build a life focused in on oneself, seeking pleasure and reward, even at the expense of others. Hope would challenge that kind of lifestyle.

Living for Others — Martin Luther King Jr.

In the midst of the American experience of the twentieth century came a black Baptist preacher, Martin Luther King Jr. He challenged the racist practices of American society through nonviolent resistance. His faith in God sustained him, even as the risk of violent backlash became apparent. His willingness to stay the course, to work toward the equality of all human beings, and to free African Americans from the remnants of slavery was a call to freedom recognized by people all over the world. He was awarded the Nobel Peace Prize in 1964. In his acceptance speech, Dr. King spoke of the struggle of the civil rights movement in the United States, the unfinished work that lay ahead, and his willingness to assume the burdens and hardships of what was next.

> I refuse to accept the cynical notion that nation after nation must spiral down a militaristic stairway into the hell of thermonuclear destruction. I believe that unarmed truth and unconditional love will have the final word in reality. This is why right temporarily defeated is stronger than evil triumphant. I believe that even amid today's mortar bursts and whining bullets, there is still hope for a brighter tomorrow. I believe that wounded justice, lying prostrate on the blood-flowing streets of our nations, can be lifted from this dust of shame to reign supreme among the

children of men. I have the audacity to believe that peoples everywhere can have three meals a day for their bodies, education and culture for their minds, and dignity, equality, and freedom for their spirits. I believe that what self-centered men have torn down men other-centered can build up. I still believe that one day mankind will bow before the altars of God and be crowned triumphant over war and bloodshed, and nonviolent redemptive good will proclaimed the rule of the land. "And the lion and lamb shall lie down together and every man shall sit under his own vine and fig tree and none shall be afraid." I still believe that We *Shall* overcome!

This faith can give us courage to face the uncertainties of the future. It will give our tired feet new strength as we continue our forward stride toward the city of freedom. When our days become dreary with low-hovering clouds and our nights become darker than a thousand midnights, we will know that we are living in the creative turmoil of a genuine civilization struggling to be born.[5]

When our nights become darker than a thousand midnights... Martin Luther King Jr. knew that the struggle for human freedom meant conflict with others unwilling to relinquish their privileged place in the community. He was inspired by the model of both Christ, who offered himself on a cross, and by Mahatma Gandhi, the spiritual leader of the Indian people in their quest to achieve freedom from British occupation. And he knew the dangers were growing, and his life was at risk. But he did not turn away from

what he felt God was calling him to do. That focus and
hope for a better future were rooted in his trust in God.
And what would American society be like today if he had
turned away, protecting himself from harm?

A Church in Solidarity

We began the chapter with St. Paul and his discussion with
the leaders of the church at Ephesus. His story parallels
that of Martin Luther King Jr. Paul accepts the burden of
preaching the gospel and the consequences of that burden. He accepts that this journey may end in his death.
And yet he persists. He believes in his mission and will
not be dissuaded from it: "I am going to Jerusalem." He
is "other-centered" and will work to undo the damage that
the self-centered inflict on others. He sees the power of God
at work in the world and chooses to be a part of it.

In the twentieth century, Catholic reflection on the
suffering of the peoples of Latin America led to the development of liberation theology. Catholic ministers, priests,
religious women, and laypeople, caring for the poor and
powerless, walked the same road as St. Paul, as Martin Luther King Jr., and as so many Christians over the
centuries. Within the cultural awakenings of democracy,
equality, and freedom a critique of Latin American politics emerged. A church that once unquestionably accepted
military dictatorships and oligarchy began to raise objec-
tions. Archbishop Oscar Romero journeyed with Martin
Luther King Jr. and proclaimed the injustice around him.
And he was killed, gunned down in church while he was

celebrating a memorial mass. The awakening of Catholics in Latin America led to the bishops' conference in Medellín, Colombia, in 1968.[6] There they fashioned a new vision for ministry in Latin America, which came to be known as the "option for the poor." The church's resources must be devoted to those in greatest need. The spirit of this move was affirmed by the Synod of Bishops Second General Assembly in their document *Justice in the World:*

> The power of the Spirit, who raised Christ from the dead, is continuously at work in the world. Through the generous sons and daughters of the Church likewise, the People of God is present in the midst of the poor and of those who suffer oppression and persecution; it lives in its own flesh and its own heart the Passion of Christ and bears witness to his resurrection.
>
> The entire creation has been groaning till now in an act of giving birth, as it waits for the glory of the children of God to be revealed (cf. Rom. 8:22). Let Christians therefore be convinced that they will yet find the fruits of their own nature and effort cleansed of all impurities in the new earth which God is now preparing for them, and in which they will be the kingdom of justice and love, a kingdom which will be fully perfected when the Lord will come himself.
>
> Hope in the coming kingdom is already beginning to take root in the hearts of men. The radical transformation of the world in the Paschal Mystery of the Lord gives full meaning to the efforts of men, and in particular of the young, to lessen injustice, violence,

and hatred and to advance all together in justice, freedom, brotherhood and love.[7]

This marked a true turning point, where the Catholic Church stood in solidarity with peoples around the world whose lives were awakened to their rights and place in the human family. That willingness to imagine a different world and to work toward it no matter the cost is the essence of hope.

A Prayer of Hope

There was a man named Max Ehrmann, who lived in Indiana early in the twentieth century. I know little else about him, other than the fact that he wrote a poem that has come to be a light for many people. It is entitled, "Desiderata." He offers comfort and consoles the willing listener with gentle advice about finding one's place in this world. He concludes by saying:

Beyond a wholesome discipline,
be gentle with yourself.
You are a child of the universe,
no less than the trees and the stars;
you have a right to be here.
And whether or not it is clear to you,
no doubt the universe is unfolding as it should.

Therefore, be at peace with God,
whatever you conceive Him to be.
And whatever your labors and aspirations,
in the noisy confusion of life, keep peace in your soul.

With all its sham, drudgery, and broken dreams;
it is still a beautiful world.
Be cheerful.
Strive to be happy.

The Origins of Evil

It's hard sometimes to imagine that the universe is indeed
"unfolding as it should." At least for the human community, the turn of the twenty-first century has already been
marred by wars and violence, by terrorist attacks, by religious hatred and tribal genocide. It's hard to imagine that
this world is following God's plan. More likely, perhaps,
would be one of the stories of the Roman gods. Legend has
it that the gods sent Pandora, a beautiful woman, to earth
as a gift.[8] Pandora became the companion of Epimetheus,
Prometheus's brother. They lived happily, until one day
Mercury arrives, heavily burdened by a box that he carried. They offer to guard the box for the night, and Mercury
hastens away. Left alone with the large box, Pandora's curiosity is piqued. And then she thinks she hears voices,
whispers, coming from the box. She fumbles with the gold
cord that keeps it shut and with her own doubts about the
rightness of opening it. The voices call her name, begging
to be released. And so she gives in. "Now, Jupiter had ma-
lignantly crammed into the box all the diseases, sorrows,
vices, and crimes that afflict poor humanity; and the box
was no sooner opened, than all these ills flew out."[9] These
ills, in the form of fluttering moths, stung Pandora and
Prometheus and flew from the house. Pandora hears another voice calling from the box, offering to heal them.

And so she releases Hope. "Thus, according to the ancients, evil entered into the world, bringing untold misery; but Hope followed closely in its footsteps, to aid struggling humanity, and point to a happier future."[10]

The legend of Pandora suggests that the gods, the divine beings that the people looked up to in the heavens, wished evil upon the human race. Pain, illness, and the human propensity for vice were conceived in the ill will of the perfect gods and inflicted upon the human race in idle cruelty. And human suffering began at the hands of a woman. The Judeo-Christian tradition held on to a similar myth, that evil came through the agency of a woman, in the account of the Fall in the book of Genesis. This impulse to direct attention to women and somehow blame them has been systematically challenged by feminist theologians and scholars in our times. According to Joan Chittister such thinking is rooted in patriarchy and its ancient fears about the power inherent in women's bodies:

> Bodies, with their drives and needs, their impulses and urges, warranted basic distrust by virtue of their threat to right reasoning, if nothing else. And women, most of all, the blatantly natural, the totally carnal, the most bodily of bodies, epitomized the hazard and jeopardized the rationality of the male soul. If men responded to the presence of a woman spontaneously, then the way to protect the soul of the man from distraction, irrationality, and sin was to keep women out of sight, out of mind. Women's bodies were dangerous to men, dangerous to thought, dangerous to society, dangerous to religion.[11]

In the legend of Pandora, Epimetheus is both startled and displeased by Pandora's curiosity, which he found unseemly.

Responding to Evil

Although the heritage of Christian thought about the origin of evil remains problematic, here we can note that Christians would argue that evil and suffering experienced by the human race were not intentionally inflicted by God. Rather, God entered fully into the human experience to heal it of its pain and suffering.[12] Christians see in the incarnation, in the union of God and human being, the truth that God loves us.

How then should Christians respond to evil? We must follow in the steps of Jesus: "If anyone wishes to come after me, he must deny himself and take up his cross daily and follow me. For whoever wishes to save his life will lose it, but whoever loses his life for my sake will save it" (Luke 9:23–24). This became a reality and a choice for Archbishop Oscar Romero. It is reported that about two weeks before his death, he said:

I have often been threatened with death. I must tell you, as a Christian, I do not believe in death without resurrection. If I am killed, I shall arise in the Salvadoran people. I say so without boasting, with the greatest humility.

As a shepherd, I am obliged by divine mandate to give my life for those I love—for all Salvadorans, even for those who may be going to kill me. If the threats are carried out, from this moment I offer my blood to God for the redemption and for the resurrection of El Salvador.

Martyrdom is a grace of God that I do not believe I deserve. But if God accepts the sacrifice of my life, let my blood be a seed of freedom and the sign that hope will soon be reality. Let my death, if it is accepted by God, be for my people's liberation and as a witness of hope in the future.

You may say, if they succeed in killing me, that I pardon and bless those who do it. Would, indeed, that they might be convinced that they will waste their time. A bishop will die, but God's church, which is in the people, will never perish.[13]

Evil cannot overcome the power of love and self-sacrifice that came alive in Jesus. Christians have come to understand that love is stronger than evil, that love must stand strong against its destructive force. It's interesting to note that Max Ehrmann wrote his poem in 1927, not an easy era and not so different from our own times. World War I was over, but not its evil effects. And surely there were forewarnings of the Depression. Perhaps, then, he was not foolish, naïve, or comfortable in his hope. Just determined.

Conclusion

Hope is born in struggle, in suffering, and pain. It is a strength, a capacity to endure that is buried deeply in the human spirit. To live an intentional life as a Christian, one is called to make the decision to live with hope. Its opposite, despair, calls at many turns in the road. In some ways, despair has earned its place in human experience as a lament against the suffering we see every day. But, to linger with despair would lead ultimately to expanding human suffering rather than ending it. Despair immobilizes; it does not inspire or empower. So hope is not naïve, but it is determined to respond to life. That determination is not rooted solely in human will, but rather also it is rooted in the Christian's experience of grace, of God with us. And with the grace, we can see the beauty and joy and gift that life is for us. And we can find some happiness. For this world and this life are good; they are God's creation. And not a malevolent god acting on a whim, but a God of light. Trusting in that God of light is the life of faith. And molding one's own life into that image of light, of light in the darkness, is the life of hope.

Chapter Three

LOVE

But to you who hear I say, love your enemies, do good to those who hate you, bless those who curse you, pray for those who mistreat you.

—Luke 6:27–28 (Sermon on the Plain)

♦ ♦ ♦

CENTRAL TO CHRISTIAN FAITH is a belief that love is God, and that to live as a Christian is to love as God loves. The model for that loving care of others is found in the person of Jesus and in the stories recalled in the New Testament that reveal his actions and teachings. Jesus' vision of what love is and what he expected his followers to do, as evidenced by the command to "love your enemies," will be explored in this chapter. How does a Christian love? And what forces would pull against one's ability to love?

Theological Foundations

What is love? That's a question that has been raised by people across time. Artists, philosophers, butchers, bakers, young, old, songwriters, and bartenders, there is hardly a person who does not have an opinion about what love means. It's a pleasant question, and it turns our attention to some of life's best experiences. Of course there are many ways to approach the question, but I'm going to turn to classical Greek notions of love that have stood the test of time, influencing many thinkers, including Christians. Love, actually, is loves, that is, four different ways that we express and experience love: libido, eros, friendship, and agape.[1]

Libido is sex drive, a force we share with animals. Society, religion, and culture set rules to govern sexual behavior. But in itself, libido is a natural urge, a sexual appetite. Eros is a desire for the beloved, the one true love. This experience of love has been expressed throughout history in poetry, prose, paintings, and music. The term attempts to describe the height and depth, the joys and despair, of this powerful and exclusive kind of love. Friendship is a bond that unites people. It brings a sense of belonging, a feeling of sharing life with others. Friendships endure through good times and bad, and form the fundamental fiber of human society. Agape is the self-gift of love, expecting nothing in return. Agape is the term Christians use to describe God's love. Human beings experience growth in their ability to love as they go through life. For ordinary people, agape is demonstrated in parenting, in mentoring, and in a loving marriage, where all four loves are expressed.[2]

Expressions of Love

Maybe love doesn't begin with sex, end with sex, or have anything to do with sex. But it is a classic starting point in describing love. We share our sex drive with other animals, except for the simple fact that humans have no "season"; our sexual desires don't wax and wane with springtime. This sexual appetite is made to conform to norms of behavior established by family, ethnic, societal, and religious expectations. The question of proper sexual conduct will be addressed later in this text when we discuss the virtue of temperance. But for now, let it suffice to note that love has a physical expression and that it is one of the ways in which we share life as a human community. Our love for one another can be expressed in physical union. The power of this intimacy and pleasure defines one aspect of the way in which we are human, the way in which our mind, body, and spirit are interconnected.

When that physical attraction intertwines with the emotions, love can be shared with complete devotion. Eros characterizes that focused love; passion is its physical expression. The willingness of the human person to marry and commit to faithfulness for a lifetime, with all of the losses and limitations that entails, must be rooted in some deep trait of the human spirit. Why deny the pleasure of new possibilities, new partners, and new experiences, if that denial did not bring a higher reward, a deeper satisfaction and meaningfulness? With all the failures of love, with the realities of divorce and infidelity, still the willingness to marry and the ideal of fidelity and companionship seem undiminished. Even in our modern, technological, secular culture, romance and love seem untainted by our many failures. The power of eros seems undiminished.

What would life be like without friends? What would life be like if we had no one with whom we could share our stories, our adventures, our successes and failures, our heartbreaks and joys? We form a human community, a network of support and solidarity. Human beings are fundamentally social creatures, bound by need and desire to live, work, play, celebrate, and mourn together. We are neighbors, co-workers, PTA members, volunteers. Charities and blood drives, political campaigns and baseball teams all depend on the willingness of one person to care for and look after the needs of others. Friendships are experienced throughout life, from early childhood to our last days.

What are the characteristics of friendship? They vary considerably, but we could say that friendship is a choice, a willingness to establish a relationship with another. Real friendships evolve over time, as shared experiences bring a greater depth of familiarity and acceptance. Friendships are rooted in common interests, pursuits, and values. They involve commitment and find their depth in shared difficulties. A true friendship is strengthened by hardships; it endures and perseveres in the face of adversity. The value of friendship cannot be underestimated. Without friends, life is a solitary road.

Love, however, reaches beyond the intimate bonds of friendship, to give and not receive in return. "Agape" refers to love that must be rooted in the divine. For why would someone stay up night after night with a sick child, or give a kidney to a stranger? Why would someone run into a burning building? There is some kind of magic in a love that is selfless. Human beings have a capacity to give of themselves, caring more for another than for themselves. On the most practical of levels, it doesn't make sense, especially to give the ultimate gift, one's life for the

sake of another. And yet the complex web of human society would fail without this selflessness. What would the
world be like if we abandoned our children? What if we
stopped caring for our elderly parents when they become
ill or burdensome? What if a marriage vow lasted only
until a new infatuation came along? What if the men and
women on the assembly line stopped making reliable cars?
Or if mail carriers delivered mail only until they started to
feel tired and then turned around and went home? What
if doctors refused to do complicated surgeries, or teachers accepted only "A" students in their classrooms? Our
humanness, the true richness and meaningfulness of life,
is dependent on the extraordinary capacity of human beings to love—beyond their own needs, their own desires,
their own reward.

The Trinity

Love, then, is loves. Libido, eros, friendship, and agape re-
fer to different dimensions of loving. These are ways in
which human beings experience love. And Christians have
claimed that God is love. The experience of Jesus' followers recorded in the New Testament opened avenues for
talking about God that were revelation, completely unknown and unexpected. They experienced Jesus calling
God Father, *Abba,* Daddy, and when the early followers
were struggling to follow in Jesus' footsteps and preach
the good news, the presence of the Holy Spirit guided and
comforted them. In their encounters with Jesus after his
resurrection, they came to believe and understand the idea

of the incarnation, that somehow Jesus was God become human.

Their experience revealed the *Trinity* in its most primitive form. Over two thousand years, the Christian community has held to a belief that God is a trinity, triune, Father, Son, and Spirit. This was incomprehensible to Judaism, which held to belief in one God in the face of the polytheism of the ancient world. Islam also proclaims the oneness of God. Christians hold to their faith in God's triune nature to be faithful to their experience of God. In the global community in which we live today, the basis for interreligious dialogue is honesty and respect for difference. Hopefully, there is a place of common ground for the religions of the "Book," even though significant differences remain. For the Catholic community, the commitment to God as triune remains inspiring and intact. The long tradition of reflection on the Trinity is exemplified by the twelfth-century spiritual writings of Richard of St. Victor.

> The perfection of one person requires fellowship with another. We have discovered that nothing is more glorious, more magnificent than to wish to have nothing that you do not wish to share. And so a person who was supremely good would not wish to be without a sharer of His majesty. However, without doubt, whatever that One whose will was omnipotent willed to exist must exist; whatever that One whose will was unchangeable once willed, He always willed. Therefore, it is necessary that an eternal person have a coeternal person, for one is not able to precede the other nor is one able to follow the other. For just as

nothing in that eternal and unchangeable Divinity is able to regress to an earlier condition, so nothing is able to come to a new condition. And so it is utterly impossible for divine persons not to be coeternal. For where there is true Divinity, there supreme goodness and full happiness exist. However, as has been said, supreme goodness cannot exist without perfect charity, nor can perfect charity exist without a plurality of persons. Indeed, full happiness cannot exist without true unchangeability, nor can true unchangeability exist without eternity. True charity demands a plurality of persons; true unchangeability demands a coeternity of persons.[3]

The perfection of God necessitates a perfect ability to love. Pure and perfect love demands equality. How could God's love be perfected in relations with human beings, who are not capable of complete union with God? The Trinity expresses complete divine love. In the course of history, Christians have always found companionship and solidarity in *community*. Christian love grows and thrives within community. The full expression of ordinary love is found in marriage and children, family and friends. The full expression of Christian love is found in a communal life of prayer, worship, and service. Christians come together to live out Jesus' command, "A new commandment I give to you, that you love one another; even as I have loved you, that you also love one another" (John 13:34). Love means community, divine and human.

A mystery remains. How can Christians love in the way that Jesus loved? It seems impossible. We need to consider what it is within human beings that would allow them to love in a way that is divine. The clue can be found in the Genesis narrative of creation, where God creates the human person: "Then God said, 'Let us make man in our image, after our likeness; and let them have dominion over the fish of the sea, and over the birds of the air, and over the cattle, and over all the earth and over every creeping thing that creeps upon the earth.' So God created man in his own image, in the image of God he created him; male and female he created them" (Genesis 1:26–27). What does it mean to be created in God's image? Being made in the image of God means having the capacity to respond to God's loving will and design for human beings. For Christians, to recall the Genesis creation story opens up a mystery — the faith of a people in a creator God, who creates and sustains all living beings—animals, plants, and people. Notwithstanding all of our scientific discoveries, the actual nature of living things remains a mystery. The claim that human beings are destined for a life with God in eternity is rooted in this belief that human beings have something in common with God's own nature. That divine spark within us is what enables us to love as God loves.

To Love as God Loves

Modern Catholic theology was inspired by the substantive changes that took place at the Second Vatican Council. These changes had been fermenting for decades before the council in response to major developments in the political, intellectual, and religious lives of the global community.

War and strife, atomic bombs and genocide, revolutions for independence from colonial rule, these all had an impact on the worldview of the Catholic community. The remarkable advances in knowledge, the formation of the disciplines of sociology and psychology, the growth of technology that began in the nineteenth century survived the wars and continued to expand. Air and space travel, medicine, and computer science developed in spite of the tremendous turmoil of these times. The rise of secular culture and the separation of church and state effected with the end of the Papal States in 1870 led to a defensive stance on the part of Catholicism vis-á-vis modern culture. The end of the twentieth century was capped by an intellectual climate that fostered a growth in historical consciousness and a turn to the subject. Truth was found within human experience. Trust in a revealed religion waned.

Primordial Will

In this climate, Maurice Blondel, a French lay Catholic philosopher and theologian, crafted an argument in defense of Catholic faith that built upon the internal workings of human "action."[4] His thinking was not well received by his philosophical colleagues in Paris when it was first presented at his doctoral defense in 1893. Nonetheless, Blondel's thinking opened avenues for new directions in Catholic thought and is counted among the many intellectual, religious, and spiritual insights that paved the way for the creative work of the Second Vatican Council.

Blondel presented an analysis of human action that opened up the possibility of transcendence, that human beings had within their mind and experience a capacity to imagine and desire the infinite. For Blondel, this was possible because human beings experienced within themselves a "primordial will," a will that called them into life and sustained them. A growing awareness of consciousness draws a person into self-probing. Why am I alive? Where am I going? Why do I feel the weight of moral responsibility on my shoulders? What will make me happy? What should I do with this life I have been given? What will happen to me at my death? These questions begin a journey toward meaning and purpose.

That meaning and purpose, Blondel argued, could be discovered when one's free will is oriented to the primordial will within oneself. Through this dynamic interrelationship between the divine and the human, the possibility opens for human transcendence. Blondel reasoned that the discovery of this primordial will occurred in living. Human action was the place for this discovery. Ordinary experience, especially the power of the human spirit to endure and overcome suffering, revealed the presence of God's living will. That will calls us into life, into relationships, into the great love of our lives, into marriage and children and friends, into a community that opens us up to the whole of the human family. The primordial will becomes a source of life and energy. How can a human will be touched and supported by a divine presence without being overpowered by it? Blondel considered human autonomy intact, unaffected by this divine presence. That divine presence remains constant, similar to the organic force of life that pushes blood through the body. It is by free human choice that one's own free will becomes aligned with the primordial will. Why make this choice? For Blondel, living in harmony with the divine will empowered individuals to live out their greatest dreams and longings, to reach for the infinite, and to trust in a destiny that would survive death.

How could a human being love the way God loves? How could Christians fulfill Jesus' command to love one another as he had loved them? Simply put, only with God's love, available within the experience and action of the human person as the primordial will. Blondel defended his Catholic faith in the face of derision and challenge. Today, his insight opens up the path of Christian virtue. For in the final analysis, to live any of the virtues necessitates the highest level of human conduct, the deepest purpose, the strongest strength of character. It seems clear, since there is ample evidence throughout human history that people have achieved these heights of virtue, that there is some kind of power within the human person that makes it possible. For people of faith, that power is from God.

To Love as Jesus Loved

The stories of Jesus' life and ministry are told in the Gospel narratives. In the Gospel of Luke, after gathering his disciples Jesus moved with them out onto a plain. Many people were gathered there. Jesus began to speak to the crowd:

> Blessed are you poor,
> for yours is the kingdom of God.
> Blessed are you that hunger now,
> for you shall be satisfied.
> Blessed are you that weep now,
> for you shall laugh....
>
> (Luke 6:20–21)

Jesus' life was filled with the sorrows of others. He reached out to the sick, the lonely, the bereaved, those whose bodies and spirits were broken. The miracles he performed were predominantly healing miracles, designed to alleviate human suffering. Many present at this sermon had probably been healed by Jesus. The future Jesus proclaimed was a future where there would be no suffering. The promise of a transformed world was consistent with the prophetic tradition of Israel: "The Spirit of the Lord God is upon me, because the Lord has anointed me to bring good tidings to the afflicted; he has sent me to bind up the brokenhearted, to proclaim liberty to the captives, and the opening of the prison to those who are bound" (Isaiah 61:1). The kingdom of God proclaimed by Jesus was realized through Jesus' own journey through suffering and death. Life would change because evil would be conquered.

In appearing to his disciples after the resurrection, Jesus called them to continue the work that he began on earth, to bring the good news of salvation, to heal and forgive sins. To do so, they must learn to love as he did, to take on evil by enduring suffering. Jesus says:

Love your enemies,
do good to those who hate you,
Bless those who curse you,
pray for those who abuse you.
To him who strikes you on the cheek,
offer the other also;
And from him who takes away your coat
do not withhold even your shirt.
Give to everyone who begs from you;
and of him who takes away your goods
do not ask them again.
And as you wish that men would do to you,
do so to them.

If you love those who love you,
what credit is that to you?
For even sinners love those who love them....
But love your enemies, and do good,
and lend, expecting nothing in return;
and your reward will be great,
and you will be sons of the Most High.

(Luke 6:27–32; 35)

The command to love is extraordinary. It goes against common sense. And it certainly has been misused and misrepresented in Christian history. What then does it mean today? Mother Teresa, a Catholic sister who devoted her life to the poorest of the poor and gathered followers who lived in complete simplicity and service, speaks of love in this way:

"Love one another, even as I have loved you." These words should be not only a light to us, but also a flame consuming the selfishness which prevents the growth of holiness. Jesus loved us to the end, to the very limit of love, the Cross. Love must come from within—from our union with Christ—an outpouring of our love for God. Loving should be as normal to us as living and breathing, day after day until our death.[5]

Love as natural as living and breathing becomes possible because the love within comes from union with Christ. For Mother Teresa, that "primordial will" within is the presence of Jesus. And as she united her love with the love of Christ, then she found that inner strength to love abundantly, fruitfully, continuously. If we look at Mother Teresa's life of service and self-sacrifice, it is clear that she found that ability to love as Jesus loved.

Love and Abuse

If theology is informed by experience, a lesson learned in Catholic thought and practice in the Vatican II era, then it needs to be said that a love that suffers for the other, even unjustly, is not the best path to manage destructive or abusive relationships. Dedication to the vows of marriage has led many women, supported by the advice of their pastors, to remain in abusive relationships. The suffering of Christ on the cross has been used to defend marital fidelity. With developments in psychology and practical care by social workers and others, it has become clear that abusive behavior or addictions cannot be cured by the sacrificial love of another. If there is going to be healing, it is a process that begins within the abusers, who must choose to change. That choice is often delayed and hampered by the "enabling" behavior of a spouse who shields them from the consequences of their addictive behavior. The partners of abusers, both men and women, can reach a state of intimidation that makes it nearly impossible for them to ask for help or freely leave the relationship.[6] Many women have been psychologically and physically hurt, even beaten and killed, by abusers who have not been confronted. Rather than interpret these situations as the responsibility of the partner, the community must step forward and commit itself to intervene.

According to Marie M. Fortune and James Poling, "The church's mistaken understanding of God's love for all people has sometimes led Christian leaders to tolerate rather than stop abusers. Providing nurturing concern and healing resources is an appropriate response for victims of violence. However, for perpetrators, the most loving response may be the development of systems of accountability and consequences that stop their destructive behaviors."[7] There is ample evidence in the life of the early church, seen in the letters of Paul, Peter, and others, that attending in an honest way to the requirements of the gospel was necessary for the health of the Christian community. Paul admonishes his followers to live according to the Spirit, whose fruits are "love, joy, peace, patience, kindness, goodness, faithfulness, gentleness, self-control" (Galatians 5:22–23), rather than their opposites, "fornication, impurity, licentiousness, idolatry, sorcery, enmity, strife, jealousy, anger, selfishness, dissension, party spirit, envy, drunkenness, carousing, and the like" (Galatians 5:19). A life of Christian faith also meant a life of Christian conduct. Being a Christian had an impact on the way one lived one's life. The Christian life was meant to be lived in community, and therefore the community should get involved when people are in trouble. In a section of the Gospel of Matthew where Jesus' parables exhort the community to care for one another and attend to the "little ones," the vulnerable, the children, Jesus suggests a method for dealing with sinful conduct:

> If your brother sins against you, go and tell him his fault, between you and him alone. If he listens to you, you have gained your brother. But if he does not listen to you, take one or two others along with you, that every word may be confirmed by the evidence of two or three witnesses. If he refuses to listen to them, tell it to the church; and if he refuses to listen even to the church, let him be to you as a Gentile and tax collector. Truly, I say to you, whatever you bind on earth shall be bound in heaven, and whatever you loose on earth shall be loosed in heaven. (Matthew 18:15–18)

It seems clear that ordinary life has its own complexities and that the web of human relationships needs its own care. That care was already at issue in the early church and is anticipated in Jesus' teachings on conflict resolution in the Gospel of Matthew. It is important to connect these principles to modern understandings of abuse and addiction, so that Christians may exercise love and wisdom.

Conclusion

The challenge for Catholics today is to love: "love the Lord your God with all your heart, and with all your soul, and with all your mind . . . [and] love your neighbor as yourself" (Matthew 22:37, 39). In this chapter we have explored the many loves of human life, and the way in which they help us understand the meaning of love. Human beings experience love divine and human. And human beings love, in divine and human ways. Maurice Blondel's notion of the primordial will allowed us to consider how it would be possible for a Christian to follow in Jesus' footsteps and love with unconditional and self-sacrificing love. When addressing the difficult question raised about abusive relationships and the call to love and forgiveness, a new virtue was identified: wisdom.

The theological virtues of faith, hope, and love became central to the Christian community in the way it defined Christian life. But along with these, the tradition included these natural virtues identified by Aristotle: prudence, justice, temperance, and fortitude. A full understanding of the nature of living a Christian life compels us to consider these natural virtues.

Part Two

The Natural Virtues

Chapter Four

PRUDENCE

Happy is the man who finds wisdom,
and the man who gets understanding,
for the gain from it is better than gain from silver
and its profit better than gold.

She is more precious than jewels,
and nothing you desire can compare with her.

Long life is in her right hand;
in her left hand are riches and honor.

Her ways are ways of pleasantness,
and all her paths are peace.
She is a tree of life to those who lay hold of her;
those who hold her fast are called happy.

—Proverbs 3:13–18

The will moves all faculties to their acts. Now the first
act of the appetitive faculty is love, as stated above (I-II,
Q. 25, AA.1,2). Accordingly prudence is said to be love,
not indeed essentially, but insofar as love moves to the
act of prudence. Wherefore Augustine goes on to say that

prudence is love discerning aright that which helps from that which hinders us in tending to God.

—St. Thomas Aquinas, *Summa Theologica,*
II-II, Q. 47, *Reply Obj.* 1.[1]

◆ ◆ ◆

LIVING A CHRISTIAN LIFE calls forth many things from a person. In the first part of this book we focused on the theological virtues of faith, hope, and love. A consideration of these virtues opened the path to understanding the fundamental expectations of anyone who would follow Jesus. In the course of time—the years, then centuries, of the life of the Christian community — other insights developed about the nature of the call to discipleship. The Christian community was heavily influenced by the heritage of Greco-Roman philosophy and Western culture. Thomas Aquinas read Aristotle's *Nicomachean Ethics,* and it influenced his understanding of the virtues. In his treatment of the virtues in the *Summa Theologica,* Aquinas turns to Christian writers, especially St. Augustine, but also relies heavily on Aristotle to structure his presentation of the virtues. The natural virtues — prudence, justice, temperance, and fortitude—became firmly embedded in Christian thinking through the work of St. Thomas Aquinas.

Prudence is "right reason in action."[2] Prudence is wise judgment, and its opposite is impulsiveness. Impulsive decisions mark a thoughtlessness that causes harm to self and others. It was understood to be the intellectual virtue, the one that organizes the other virtues.

Theological Reflection

Another way to capture the essence of prudence is to consider its heart: wisdom. There is a strong religious heritage in the Scriptures about wisdom. The Old Testament contains many folkways, tidbits of advice about appropriate conduct for living a good life. For example, in the book of Proverbs: "Happy the man who finds wisdom" (Proverbs 3:13). References to wisdom are personified in the Old Testament. Wisdom is present at creation. In the book of Proverbs, wisdom is "she." Elizabeth Johnson has explored the possibilities of what this wisdom tradition might mean.[3] She notes that in Proverbs 8, "The Discourse of Wisdom," Wisdom preexists the earth and is "begotten." This has led to theological speculation about Wisdom as the Spirit, the third person of the Trinity. Elisabeth Schüssler Fiorenza takes up the theme of Divine Sophia in her text *Jesus: Miriam's Child, Sophia's Prophet:*

> Divine Sophia has her residence in heaven. She is the glory of G*d (Wisd. 7:25–26), mediator of creation (Wisd. 8:5–6), and shares the throne of G*d (Wisd. 9:3). She rules over kings and is herself all powerful. She makes everything, and permeates the cosmos (Wisd. 7:23, 27; 8:1, 5). "She is but one, yet can do everything; herself unchanging, she makes all things new" (Wisd. 7:27). She is "intelligent and holy, free moving, clear, loving what is good, eager, beneficent, unique in her Way." (Wisd. 7:22)[4]

The mystery of Wisdom as portrayed in the Old Testament opens up possibilities for imagining and interpreting the meaning of the virtue of prudence for human beings. It seems that Wisdom is within God's very nature, a power and center of identity. To grow in wisdom, then, may be to come closer to our divine destiny. Perhaps the most familiar tradition regarding wisdom in the Old Testament is that of Solomon, King David's son, who inherits his kingdom. King Solomon asked the prophet for wisdom, which God granted. Solomon's reign was characterized by his judgment and fairness, his wisdom (1 Kings 3:1–14).

In the New Testament, the book of Acts records the conversations at a meeting in Jerusalem, a council called to address the question of whether new gentile converts to Christianity should be required to conform to Mosaic law. It was a critical question for the early church as its evangelical efforts spread beyond Judaism. The community gathered in Jerusalem, and Peter, Barnabas, and Paul told stories of their experiences baptizing gentiles. They reflected together on the problem. Finally, James, the head of the church in Jerusalem, brought the meeting to a conclusion by supporting the work of Peter, Barnabas, and Paul and allowing gentiles to become Christians without becoming Jews. In a letter sent out to the churches, they report the decision by stating:

> Since we have heard that some persons from us have troubled you with words, unsettling your minds, although we gave them no instructions, it has seemed good to us, having come to one accord, to choose men and send them to you with our beloved Barnabas and Paul, men who have risked their lives for the sake of our Lord Jesus Christ. We have therefore

sent Judas and Silas, who themselves will tell you the same things by word of mouth. For it has seemed good to the Holy Spirit and to us to lay upon you no greater burden than these necessary things: that you abstain from what has been sacrificed to idols and from blood and from what is strangled and from unchastity. If you keep yourselves from these, you will do well. Farewell. (Acts 15:24–29)

This decision in the book of Acts provides a window into the life of the early church and certainly gives evidence that successful community life involved intelligent conversation and problem-solving.

Love of the Truth

The Second Vatican Council articulated a new vision of ecumenism and interreligious dialogue. The foundation of that vision was expressed in the document on religious liberty, where the bishops state that "every human person has a right to religious freedom."[5] That freedom is rooted in a fundamental responsibility:

All men are bound to seek the truth, especially in what concerns God and his Church, and to embrace it and hold on to it as they come to know it.

The sacred Council likewise proclaims that these obligations bind man's conscience. Truth can impose itself on the mind of man only in virtue of its own truth, which wins over the mind with both gentleness and power.[6]

Seeking the truth emerges as the principle that guides individual discernment. When we consider the virtue of prudence, it seems clear that the Catholic community expects individuals to use their intellect, to think, study, pray, and develop deeper insights into the meaning of their own lives, their purpose on earth, and their relationship with God. Catholics are challenged to read and study, to participate in lectures and retreats, to read the Bible, to learn about the great theologians and saints of the tradition. To arrive at an understanding of the Truth is an intellectual journey, one marked by care and attention to the work it entails. Why is study necessary? It seems clear that the complexity of ordinary life demands it. In fact, Catholic religious orders of women and men have established colleges and universities around the world, where practical knowledge and skills are taught along with philosophy and theology.

History has had an impact on the growth and communal knowledge of society, but it has also affected Christianity. Cardinal John Henry Newman (1801–90), a great intellectual and apologist of the nineteenth century, considered the historical nature of the development of Christian doctrine:

> The increase and expansion of the Christian Creed and Ritual, and the variations which have attended the process in the case of individual writers and churches, are the necessary attendants on any philosophy or polity which takes possession of the intellect and heart and has had any wide or extended

dominion;...from the nature of the human mind, time is necessary for the full comprehension and perfection of great ideas.[7]

For Newman, the experience of the followers of Jesus artic-ulated in the New Testament, as well as that of Christians from generation to generation, needed time and reflection to come to a truer understanding of the meaning of Chris-tianity. And we can see the power of history in our own lives. We are born as helpless infants and must learn lan-guage and motor skills. From those primitive beginnings we must become fully human. To be human is to be alive, to be self-aware, to exercise our wills, emotions, and in-tellect, to become conscious of the past, the present, and the future simultaneously in our minds, to question and probe the meaning of life, to become devoted to others, and to make a place in this world. As we see our lives un-fold, we see ourselves changing. Not only do our bodies change, ebbing and then flowing away in one tidal sweep, but we see the deepening of our own grasp of the Truth. Seeing the Truth is the quest of a lifetime, the burden of every person, the joy and gift of every person. By under-standing the reality of this search, the Catholic bishops were able to defend the freedom of this journey for all people.

Religious Tolerance

The Vatican II declaration on religious freedom also al-lowed for new possibilities of interreligious dialogue and mutual respect. In the more than forty years since the conclusion of Vatican II, there has been much progress among Christians in ecumenical efforts and significant advancements in interreligious dialogue. One of the most significant contributors to Catholic life and thought, Jesuit theologian Karl Rahner, articulated the idea of the "anonymous Christian." The exclusive claim so often associated with Christianity, that orthodox Christian belief is required for salvation, was challenged by Rahner's concept that individuals lived an "implicit Christianity" if the universal gift of God's grace had been "existentially accepted in faith and love."[8] Those truth-seekers who come to recognize the gift of life in God and who follow the virtuous path share their journey with Christians. The idea of implicit Christianity assumes the best of people and the possibility that anyone could indeed be carrying on the love and ministry of Christ.

Raimundo Panikkar (b. 1918) has been "one of the leading figures in interreligious dialogue over the past half-century."[9] His intellectual and personal lives span two worlds, the tradition of Western Catholicism and ordained priesthood, and the spiritual and cultural heritage of Hinduism. His life has been dedicated to bridging the gaps between the two worlds. I remember talking with him one afternoon at a conference at Fordham University in New York. He told me that he had taken issue with Rahner's concept of anonymous or implicit Christianity, and told Rahner that he would accept it only if Rahner would acknowledge himself as an "anonymous Hindu." Scholars of Hinduism note that its rich religious tradition has been known for its openness to a diversity of beliefs, and rather identifies its specificity by proper adherence to Hindu practices.[10] Wisdom is celebrated in Hinduism's main religious text, the Bhagavad-Gita.

> Absolute joy beyond the senses
> can only be grasped by understanding;
> when one knows it, he abides there
> and never wanders from this reality.
>
> Obtaining it, he thinks
> there is no greater gain;
> abiding there, he is unmoved,
> even by deep suffering.[11]

There is no greater gain in life than to achieve wisdom.

Islam had from its foundation a recognition of and respect for members of other religions. In *The Heart of Islam,* Seyyed Hossein Nasr quotes a surah in the Quran that states "verily, those who have faith [in what is revealed to the Prophet] and those who are Jews and Christians and Sabaeans—whosoever has faith in God and the Last Day and does right—surely their reward is with their Lord, and no fear shall overcome them and neither shall they grieve (2:62)."[12] The Jewish people in Spain during the Muslim era of control enjoyed great intellectual and religious freedom. And in the modern era, in Rwanda during the horrific genocidal war waged by the Hutus against both Tutsis and moderate Hutus, the Muslim community harbored fugitives and saved many lives.[13]

Buddhism also invites respect for other beings. The Dalai Lama writes:

> The four virtuous actions.... The first is never to lie to any living being. There are a few exceptions where you might have to tell lies in order to protect the Dharma or other people, but otherwise you should avoid telling lies to anybody. The second virtuous action is to be honest, and the third is to praise and have high regard for bodhisattvas, who are constantly working for others. Again, it is very difficult to assess who is and who is not a bodhisattva, so it is safer to develop a strong sense of respect toward all sentient beings and always speak highly of them and praise their positive qualities. The fourth virtuous action is exhorting others to work for the achievement of Buddhahood, the completely enlightened state.[14]

In the world of the twenty-first century, there is room for hope. For in spite of the devastating realities of religious hatred and violence, the foundational principles of these great religions show mutual respect and tolerance. And of course the central teaching of Judaism, embedded in the Torah, is the protection of the "widow, orphan, and stranger among you." As strangers together, across cultures, races, and religions, we share this common journey: to seek the Truth. We turn now to the questions: How do we find that truth? How do we become wise?

Becoming Wise

How is it that one becomes wise? For if the purpose of learning about the virtues is to live them, then surely there have to be clues to discern the path. If there were a key to unlocking the door to wisdom, it seems to me that it would be *knowing that time passes.* There is an Irish folk song, "A Bunch of Thyme," whose verse reads:

> Time brings all things to my mind,
> time it is a precious thing,
> with all its labors along with all its joys,
> and time brings all things to an end.

Why do we think wisdom is achieved in old age? Perhaps it is because those who have lived a long time have experienced many things, and through those experiences they have come to grasp the reality of time. Time is moving constantly, pushing life forward. One day you are a child, the next day you are grown. One day you are starting your marriage, and the next day you are grieving at a grave. The good and the bad, the successes and failures, the most important and the least important, all this changes constantly. Time is relentless. Perhaps it is a harsh teacher, but for those willing to learn, it has much to say. Life has a beginning and an end. Actions have consequences. Some problems cannot be solved. Some wounds cannot heal. Today will never come again.

The young sometimes learn this lesson if they are forced to look at time in the eye. Young Mattie J. T. Stepanek was such a one. He was born with a particularly debilitating form of muscular dystrophy. The disease claimed the lives of his two brothers and sister. In his short life, Mattie was able to reach out to the world and speak his truth. He wrote poetry and proclaimed his dreams for world peace.

He became a spokesperson, a dreamer, and a model of courage and hopefulness. One of his poems was entitled, "When I Die (Part II)."

> When I die, I want to be
> A child in Heaven.
> I want to be
> A ten-year-old cherub.
> I want to be
> A hero in Heaven.
> And a peacemaker,
> Just like my goal in earth.
> I will ask God if I can
> Help the people in purgatory.
> I will help them think,
> About their life,
> About their spirits,
> About their future.
> I will help them
> Hear their Heartsongs again,
> So they can finally
> See the face of God,
> So soon.
> When I die,
> I want to be
> Just like I want to be
> Here on earth.
>
> —November 1999[15]

Mattie Stepanek died in June 2004. He was thirteen years old.

Conclusion

The world has changed since those times of optimism and fear, the optimism at the end of World War II and the fear of nuclear weapons that drove the international community to form the United Nations and inspired the leader of the Catholic Church to call the Second Vatican Council. Charles Dickens wrote, "It was the best of times, it was the worst of times." We are in the best of times and the worst of times, a time of terrorism and fear, and a time of unprecedented potential for global solidarity. It's hard to read the future, hard to know what will happen next. But we must undertake the task before us. To be a Catholic today is to seek the truth, to look for wisdom in the midst of troubled times.

Chapter Five

JUSTICE

The scribes and the Pharisees brought a woman who had been caught in the act of adultery, and placing her in the midst they said to him, "Teacher, this woman has been caught in the act of adultery. Now in the law Moses commanded us to stone such. What do you say about her?" This they said to test him, that they might have some charge to bring against him. Jesus bent down and wrote with his finger on the ground. And as they continued to ask him, he stood up and said to them, "Let him who is without sin among you be the first to throw a stone at her." And once more he bent down and wrote with his finger on the ground. But when they heard it, they went away, one by one, beginning with the eldest. And Jesus was left alone with the woman standing before him. Jesus looked up and said to her, "Woman, where are they? Has no one condemned you?" She said, "No one, Lord." And Jesus said, "Neither do I condemn you; go, and sin no more."

—John 8:1–11

Man's dealings with himself are sufficiently rectified by the rectification of the passions by the other moral virtues. But his dealings with others need a special rectification,

*not only in relation to the agent, but also in relation to
the person to whom they are directed. Hence about such
dealings there is a special virtue, and this is justice.*

—St. Thomas, *Summa Theologica,* II-II, Q. 58, *Reply Obj.* 4

♦ ♦ ♦

T HE ISSUE OF JUSTICE raises a fundamental question:
What are the right relationships between persons in
a society? The answer to this question is heavily influenced by culture, religion, politics, and history. A person
lives justly, or not, within a given national identity, socio-
cultural set of expectations, and time of history that poses
its own challenges and demands. Unlike the other virtues,
just conduct is always relational. It is the way in which
we act in community. To be just is by nature to be just to
others. In a pluralistic society, where there coexist com-
peting worldviews, it becomes very difficult to determine
"right conduct" that is universally true.

Twentieth-century American concepts of justice have
been articulated in politics, sociology, and philosophy, and
implemented in the court systems. Many have argued that
the heart of American concepts of justice is the protection of individual freedom. The center of American justice
is the protection of the rights of the individual. It can
be seen in the aggressive separation of church and state,
legalized abortion, and the competitive, capitalistic principles of the economy, which largely ignore the poor and
marginalized. The poor, it is said, are themselves to blame
because they refuse to comply with the rules of capitalistic success — self-advancement through education, hard

work, and perseverance. Anyone can succeed in America, or so goes the myth. But what is a Christian concept of justice?

Theological Reflection

Inherited concepts of justice were well established at the time of Jesus. The worldview, cult, economy, mores, and values of ancient Jewish society were articulated in the laws of Israel. We began the chapter with a story about Jesus and the woman caught in adultery. The people knew the punishment — stoning. Jesus challenged the law and invited those present to consider a more compassionate approach, to see themselves as sinners, too, and offer everyone a chance to live and live differently.

From where we stand today, it seems clear that the early church needed to distinguish itself from Judaism. The decision of the Jerusalem Council showed that the church was moving away from its Jewish roots. This path led to a great deal of rancor and suffering among the Jewish community, which endured the destruction of the Temple by Rome and subsequent oppression. Christians were excommunicated from the synagogue in 95 C.E. In the same period, Rome also turned on the new church, as Emperor Nero accused the Christians of setting the city on fire and began a period of persecution of Christians. The first Christian martyrs died before the century was over. In his letter to the Romans Paul contrasted the "old" Law of Israel and the "new" Law of Christianity and justified Christianity's superior morality and justice: "for the law of the Spirit of life in Christ Jesus has set me free from the law of sin and death"

(Romans 8:2). Paul's concept of the new law in the Spirit had enormous impact on Christianity's self-definition.

The task for us today is to articulate how Christians define right relationships and just lives. And would it be possible to define the virtue of justice without reconnecting with the historical tradition that portrays Christian morality as superior to the law of Israel?

Kathryn Tanner, a professor of Christian theology at the University of Chicago, addresses the question of the nature of the human person. She returned to the Old Testament narratives in Genesis and to the passage that stated that the human being was "made in the image and likeness of God" (Genesis 1:26).

> To be created in the image of God means, in other words, to have a particular vocation, one of fellowship and communion with God in which one uses all one's powers to glorify God and carry out God's purposes. Human beings may be alone among God's creatures in rendering conscious praise in word and deed for God's blessings in their own lives and throughout creation.... Human beings reflect God by adopting God's own universal project of well-being. Like the shepherd kings of antiquity, they mediate God's blessings, as best they are able, to both their own kind and the rest of creation — for example, replenishing the earth and helping it body forth bountifully, furthering the prospects for the human community by protecting and caring for the weak, infirm, and the oppressed.[1]

Tanner then develops key principles that emerge from this understanding of the human person. Human justice must be in harmony with God's justice. God wills the well-being of all, the human race, all the creatures of earth, and the earth itself. All of this is God's creation and deserving of its destiny to flourish. Human justice must implement God's justice in the world, must protect and care for all of life and nature. For Christians, then, there is no limit to justice. For those who have been hurt—the poor, the marginalized, the earth burdened by human waste and abuse—the Christian has the vocation to right the wrongs of the human race.

To love as God loves means to love abundantly. When we think of boundless human love, our minds move easily to the love a parent gives to a child. Self-gift and self-sacrifice characterize the level of effort necessary for a child's needs to be met. If the human person must respond to the needs of the whole human family, then that boundless love extends beyond the immediate family to envelop the human and natural worlds.

Tanner's challenge to adopt "God's own universal project of well-being" connects to the Catholic teachings on social justice. The twentieth-century developments in Catholic thought on justice in the modern world actually begin with *Rerum Novarum,* Pope Leo XIII's 1891 encyclical on the rights of the worker. The Catholic understanding of justice as expressed in official church documents builds through the end of the century to a vision of justice that can claim to be true to this vision of God's project. The social teachings that emerged included a new call, that the church must focus its energy, resources, and ministry on the most vulnerable. From the Latin American theology of the time came the idea of the "option for the poor." From Catholic ethical theory came the idea of "social sin," that injustice becomes embedded in the government, economies, laws, and policies, affecting future generations. To combat injustice, the church calls upon the Christian community to address social sin. Pope Paul VI stated it simply: "If you want peace, work for justice."

A Catholic Vision of the Human Person

Cardinal Joseph Bernardin (1928–96) served as the archbishop of Chicago and found his way into the heart of the city with his gentle demeanor and deep spirituality. When diagnosed with the cancer that eventually claimed his life, he shared his journey with openness and wisdom. He earned the respect of a wide range of people and has had a lasting influence on the Catholic community in the United States. He was an articulate spokesperson for a "consistent ethic of life."

> If one contends, as we do, that the right of every fetus to be born should be protected by civil law and supported by civil consensus, then our moral, political, and economic responsibilities do not stop at the moment of birth. Those who defend the right of life of the weakest among us must be equally visible in support of the quality of life of the powerless among us: the old and the young, the hungry and the homeless, the undocumented immigrant and the unemployed worker. Such a quality of life posture translates into

specific political and economic positions on tax policy, employment generation, welfare policy, nutrition
and feeding programs, and health care. Consistency
means we cannot have it both ways. We cannot urge
a compassionate society and vigorous public policy
to protect the rights of the unborn and then argue
that compassion and significant public programs on
behalf of the needy undermine the moral fiber of the
society or are beyond the proper scope of governmen-
tal responsibility.[2]

Bernardin argued that an ethic of life had to encompass
the whole journey of the human person, from the beginning of life through all its stages, even through diminished
capacity or illness, regardless of a person's social place,
moral conduct, or usefulness to society. In public speeches
and through his committee work for the U.S. bishops,
Cardinal Bernardin spoke with concern about American
policies on abortion, capital punishment, and euthana-
sia. In an address at Georgetown University in September
1996 he spoke of his own impending death and the lessons
about life that it was teaching him.

As a bishop, I have tried, in season and out of season, to shape and share a moral message about the
unique value of human life and our common responsibilities for it. As my life now slowly ebbs away, as
my temporal destiny becomes clearer each hour and
each day, I am not anxious, but rather reconfirmed
in my conviction about the wonder of human life, a
gift that flows from the very being of God and is en-

trusted to each of us. It is easy in the rush of daily life or in its tedium to lose the sense of wonder that is appropriate to this gift. It is even easier at the level of our societal relations to count some lives as less valuable than others, especially when caring for them costs us—financially, emotionally, or in terms of time, effort, and struggle.

The truth is, of course, that each life is of infinite value. Protecting and promoting life — caring for it and defending it — is a complex task in social and policy terms. I have struggled with the specifics often and have sensed the limits of reason in the struggle to know the good and do the right. My final hope is that my efforts have been faithful to the truth of the gospel of life and that you and others like you will find in this gospel the vision and strength needed to promote and nurture the great gift of life God has shared with us.[3]

Compassionate justice, as Jesus lived and proclaimed to those who would listen, seems clearly needed in our own times. And it answers the question, What is a Christian understanding of justice? The virtue of justice leads us on a path of day-to-day decision making, which attends to the people around us. Intentional living means that we see the invisible, hear the silent, touch the unreachable. It is a bar set higher perhaps than any of us could ever clear. But the fascinating thing is that Jesus set that bar two thousand years ago, and people from one generation to the next continue to take up the challenge.

Catholic Christians stand in solidarity with people around the world, within other religious traditions, cultures, and societies, who attend to the needs of the whole community. Reading the biographies and memoirs of Eleanor Roosevelt, the crafter of the United Nations Declaration of Human Rights, a text that emerged from the dust of World War II as a demand for a better world, we can see the difference one person's perseverance, one person's character can make in the world. It was Eleanor Roosevelt's personal efforts that led to the creation and passage of that declaration. She herself expressed confidence in the individual's ability to influence the course of human history.

> Where, after all, do universal human rights begin? In small places, close to home — so close and so small that they cannot be seen on any maps of the world. Yet they *are* the world of individual persons; the neighborhood he lives in; the school or college he attends; the factory, farm, or office where he works. Such are the places where every man, woman, and child seeks equal justice, equal opportunity, equal dignity without discrimination. Unless these rights have meaning there, they have little meaning anywhere. Without concerned citizen action close to home, we shall look in vain for progress in the larger world.[4]

The vision of a united community standing together with a common understanding of the rights of every person inspired this declaration and led to its passage by the United Nations in 1948. What if Eleanor Roosevelt had decided that one person could not make a difference, that it was impossible to achieve consensus among so many different cultures and nations?

Conclusion

A consideration of the virtue of justice involves the fundamental principles that order human relationships. A life of Christian virtue extends beyond one's own spiritual and personal beliefs, to be implemented in the world, in one's relationships. In harmony with broader Christian teachings, Catholics affirm their special responsibilities to the entire world, the living ecosystem that is God's gift to humanity.

Chapter Six

TEMPERANCE

"All things are lawful for me," but not all things are helpful. "All things are lawful for me," but I will not be enslaved by anything. —1 Corinthians 6:12

*Augustine says (*De Morib. Eccl. *xxi): "In both Testaments the temperate man finds confirmation of the rule forbidding him to love the things of this life, or to deem any of them desirable for their own sake, and commanding him to avail himself of those things with the moderation of a user, not the attachment of a lover, insofar as they are requisite for the needs of this life and of his station...."* *Now all the pleasurable objects that are at man's disposal are directed to some necessity of this life as to their end. Wherefore temperance takes the need of this life, as the rule of the pleasurable objects of which it makes use, and uses them only for as much as the need of this life requires.*

—St. Thomas Aquinas, *Summa Theologica*, II-II, Q. 141, art. 6.

◆ ◆ ◆

BY TURNING TO TEMPERANCE at this point in our discussion, we have deviated from the traditional order of the natural virtues. Aquinas positions temperance as the last of the virtues, after fortitude. I prefer to position it second to last. Regardless, the Christian tradition has placed considerable importance on controlling one's passions and appetites as one aspect of practicing the Christian faith. If this is the case, then several questions arise. What is the spiritual purpose of disciplining the body? If there is a worthy purpose, what are the practices used to achieve this kind of self-discipline?

There is ample evidence in society today of a bent toward self-destructiveness. The eating disorders of anorexia and bulimia, alcohol and substance abuse, and smoking are examples of destructive behaviors that are eroding the fabric of life and relationships and do tremendous damage to one's body. Self-indulgent behaviors, such as engaging in irresponsible sex or overeating, also impact our lives as a community. These complex social realities pose serious problems to ourselves, our friends, and our families, and dominate American life. These patterns of self-destruction should be the concern of all thoughtful people.

Why these self-destructive practices are so prevalent in modern society is a question that can be answered only within a larger framework of human experience and knowledge. The fields of psychology, medicine, sociology, and social work are where insight and correction should be found. A Christian response should fall in line with the wisdom of these professions and offer hope and encouragement to those who seek another path. Given the significant influence of these self-destructive behaviors, it could be argued that a spiritual way of living involves a different attitude toward one's body.

Theological Reflection

When we consider the ideals of Christian life, Jesus' sermons recorded in the Gospels come to mind. Jesus preached a simple lifestyle, sharing goods in common, taking only what you need, trusting God to provide what is needed, not hoarding wealth while others are in need. Images of God's bountiful providence are described. God's bountifulness can be seen in the beauty of nature, in the way in which God answers prayers. Jesus invites those who are listening to find happiness in a simple life: "Therefore I tell you, do not be anxious about your life, what you shall eat or what you shall drink, nor about your body, what you shall put on. Is not life more than food, and the body more than clothing?" (Matthew 6:25). These comments fall within a long passage in Matthew known as the Sermon on the Mount. In it, Jesus spoke of how to live what we would call the *spiritual life*.

From a Christian perspective, ordinary life is not so ordinary. Beneath the day-to-day duties, responsibilities, joys, and sorrows of human life, there lies a deeper meaning. Living means living in a web of relationships, in communion with the Divine Creator. There is more to life than food or drink or clothing, houses or cars or beach vacations. Human beings have a divine destiny, and that destiny unfolds through the passage of time on earth. In the previous chapter we discussed compassionate justice as the way in which a human person lives within relationships. How is it that anyone could live a life inspired and expressed by the virtues of faith, hope, love, prudence, justice, temperance, and fortitude? A life of integrity and purpose does not come without effort. How could it? Jesus tried to guide his followers toward a higher life, one that would be celebrated and received by his father in heaven. A spiritual life—what is it? Prayer and service form its core, as well as reflection and study.

Christians today continue to engage in spiritual disciplines established by Jesus. Jesus expected his followers to fast. This practice they inherited from Judaism. He wanted no melodrama, long faces and hungry looks so that everyone could be impressed by their self-sacrifice. Rather they should keep their fasting secret (Matthew 6:16–18). And Jesus expected them to pray, not only to participate in the public worship of the Temple and Scripture study in the synagogues, but to be committed to private prayer. And when asked, he taught them a new prayer. Don't "heap words as the Gentiles do," he said, for God knows what you need. Rather pray in this fashion:

> Our Father, who art in heaven,
> hallowed be thy name.
> Thy kingdom come.
> Thy will be done,
> on earth as it is in heaven.
> Give us this day our daily bread;
> and forgive us our debts,
> as we also have forgiven our debtors;
> and lead us not into temptation,
> but deliver us from evil.
>
> (Matthew 6:9–13)

For Jesus, prayer was proclaiming the holiness of the Creator and placing oneself before the Giver of Life, who knows our needs. Forgiveness and compassion are gifts both received from God and given to one another. Praise and supplication, speaking our needs, are the essence of this simple prayer.

In the long history of Christian spirituality fundamental characteristics have persisted: prayer, fasting, reflection and study, and service. Lifestyles emerged that persist to this day. Individual Christians became monks, living in deserted places, centering their very existence on prayer and fasting. *The Life of Saint Anthony,* written by St. Athanasius, is a celebration of this Christian way of life. The *Rule of Saint Benedict,* written in the sixth century, capsulizes monasticism as a communal life for religious, whose vows of celibacy, poverty, and obedience formed a central expression of Christian spirituality.[1] The influence of monastic spirituality on the formation of Christian life and practice cannot be underestimated.

Monks in Ireland in the same era were called upon as spiritual advisors and mentors for the Irish people, leading to a revolutionary shift from the severe penitential rituals of reconciliation introduced in the early centuries of Christianity, to a transformed, individual confessional practice of reconciliation for the development of the soul. Monastic spirituality fulfilled the goals set by Christ, to live a life of service to the community, in communion with God. Monasteries were centers of learning, spiritual and physical healing, and hospitality, and in times of political turmoil in the West they served in even larger capacities. The Rule of St. Benedict incorporated structured hours of prayer, the recitation of the Psalms of the Old Testament, and *lectio divina,* the reading and meditation on spiritual texts, balanced with simple meals, manual labor, and adequate sleep. In the early formation of Christian spirituality, as evidenced in the monastic movement, prayer and service were enhanced by a disciplined use of the body. Fasting and abstinence were seen to harness the energy of the person, where it could be focused on the one true purpose in life, to serve God.

Of course not every Christian chose this path. Parallel traditions emerged, and prayer, fasting, reflection and study, and service found other expressions in Christian life. For those who had neither the time nor ability to recite all 150 psalms in a day, the Lord's Prayer took their place. Knots were tied on a string, as counting beads, so that one could recite the Lord's Prayer 150 times in the day. The great tradition of the Rosary developed in the eleventh century, where the counting of beads now was united with the mysteries of the life of Mary and the journey of salvation through Christ. Christians gathered in church to participate in liturgies of the Word and to celebrate the Eucharist. The seasons of the life of the Christian church evolved, with Lent taking center stage in the proper self-preparation for the coming of the Easter mysteries. The rituals of confession, absolution, and penance were practiced with regularity. Charity was considered essential in following in the footsteps of Jesus. And the secular nature of marriage was slowly transformed, as the church began to see the depth of spirituality expressed through married love. Chastity, fidelity, and devotion to family were expected of the marriage partners. Thus we see a unity in purpose of Christian life, either religious or lay, in making the body serve the mind and will of the believer.

Spirituality from a World Perspective

When we look at the world's religious traditions, cross-
ing centuries and cultures, we see common characteristics.
Centering prayer is at the heart of Buddhist spirituality.
The Dalai Lama, spiritual leader of Tibetan Buddhism,
presents the fundamental principle of enlightenment:

> We can achieve enlightenment only through the
> practice of meditation; without it there is no way
> we can transform our minds. The whole purpose of
> reading or listening to Buddhist teachings is to en-
> able us to undertake the practice properly. Therefore,
> we should try our best to put what we understand
> into practice. At this juncture we have obtained this
> precious life as free and fortunate human beings,
> able to engage in this practice. We should seize the
> opportunity. Although it is important to take care
> of our livelihood, we should not be obsessed by that
> alone. We should also think of our future, for life after
> death is something we know little about and our fate
> is unpredictable. If there is a life after death, then it is
> very important to think about it and prepare for it. At
> this point, when we have obtained all the conditions
> necessary for practicing the Dharma, the teachings
> of the Buddha, we should concentrate all our efforts
> on doing so and make our lives meaningful thereby.[2]

Prayer is at the heart of the way Buddhists perceive life, relate to others, define meaning, and create direction in their
lives. Mind and body unite in common purpose through
meditation:

Fasting and alms-giving characterize the religious celebration of the month of Ramadan in Islam. The month of Ramadan was the month of the descent of the Quran. In this holiest of Islamic months, Muslims combine physical and psychological purification with an intensification of prayer, recitation of the Quran, and acts of charity. During this month, in almost all Islamic cities, vast amounts of food are provided free for the poor, and the cost of the one meal that one and one's family does not eat each day is given to the needy....

It is a time for great self-discipline and the practice of the virtues of patience and persistence in hardship for the sake of God. It is also a time to develop greater compassion toward the needy and to realize what it means to suffer from hunger.[3]

In the spirituality of Islam, these two acts of spiritual self-discipline, fasting and almsgiving, both celebrate the revelations of Mohammed and are centering acts of per-fecting Islamic religious practice.

So perhaps we can claim that there is a universality to spiritual self-discipline. The body is an instrument of the will rather than the opposite, where the person lives at the beck and call of his or her appetites. What makes us human is our ability to choose. We follow our appetites, or we choose not to do so. A mother without enough money for food will feed her children first. Even if she feels the pangs of hunger, she sees a greater duty. She has the power to override the appetite for a greater good. The body serves the will.

Self-Discipline Gone Awry

When we began this consideration of the virtues, we looked at the way in which Aristotle defined courage, as a mean between two extremes. Our intellectual strengths must guide our practice of the virtues. Otherwise, we may err in directions leading to excess, a violation of the foundational principles of a virtuous life. The past and present practice of religion shows clear evidence of the extreme misuse of the body for religious purposes. *A Treatise on the Spiritual Life,* a spiritual manual from the seventeenth century, points to the "marks" that a person had committed himself, or herself we can assume, to a spiritual life. One mark was "avoidance and contempt of honors, riches, pleasures and all things temporal. For the human heart cannot be without love and delight: therefore, he who hates the world, and its glory and delights, betrays a love of divine things and delight in the Lord."[4] To hate the world was to love the Christian life. According to this spiritual manual, it was not possible to divide one's devotion between this world and the next. Therefore, love of God was evidenced by a hatred for ordinary life.

The strength of this position lies in the truth that Jesus did indeed express similar sentiments: "Whoever loves father or mother more than me is not worthy of me; and whoever loves son or daughter more than me is not worthy of me; and whoever does not take up his cross and follow me is not worthy of me. Whoever finds his life will lose it, and whoever loses his life for my sake will find it" (Matthew 10:37–39). The weakness of this position is that it creates paths of behavior that lead to extremism, rituals of self-inflicted pain, self-righteousness, and isolation. Hatred of this world for the sake of the next has led to religious extremism in the form of suicide bombing. Hatred for the world translates into hatred for human life, a complete contradiction to the Christian belief, shared by the other religions of the Book, that life is a gift from God.

The experience of Christians today is a credible source of insight into understanding the life of faith. The lifestyle of vowed religious today, like those of the Order of St. Benedict, seek a balance in their stance to the world. "Hating the world" has not lasted in the experience of vowed religious life. And we can only hope that will be the case for other examples of violent religious extremism.

Temperance in Our Times

The question for us, then, is this: What could the virtue of temperance mean today? What is the path of self-discipline that is part of the Christian life? We have seen that the idea of a spiritual life within Catholic Christianity has included teachings about the care and discipline of one's body. But Catholic understandings of the body may be too narrowly conceived. At least that is the challenge set forth by Sallie McFague in her book *The Body of God.* In developing her thesis of the world as the body of God, she points to the teachings of the First Vatican Council of the Catholic Church and the way in which it defines the nature of God:

> ...the one true living God, Creator and Lord of Heaven and earth, almighty, eternal, immense, incomprehensible, infinite in intelligence, in will, and

in all perfection, who, as being one, sole, absolutely simple and immutable spiritual substance, is to be declared as really and essentially distinct from the world, of supreme beatitude in and from himself, and ineffably exalted above all things beside himself which exist or are conceivable.[5]

McFague argues that "it's difficult to imagine how a God so described could have a genuine, significant relationship with anything outside the divine reality."[6] McFague is arguing for another model, that of

God as the spirit of the body, the life or breath within the entire universe. Moreover, the Christic shape of this body has defined and particularized it further, in ways that have radicalized God's immanence. Divine immanence is empowerment toward liberation, well-being, and fulfillment of all the bodies within God's body.... It is this immanence, especially as expanded to include all of nature, that we have stressed in our model, not only because it has been neglected in Christianity, but also because it is what is needed in our own times.[7]

What is needed in our times? I agree that we need a sense of the holiness of nature that encompasses the immensity of the universe, all of its creatures, and the human body itself. Temperance is inspired by the gift of life, the gift of bodiliness, as life is shared in an ecosystem of union with nature. The Incarnation is both symbolic and demonstrative of the union of the divine and the human. Vatican I goes on to state that the transcendent God, with no need for us, freely brought into existence the created order and the human person, composed of spirit and body, and concludes that "everything that God has brought into being he protects and governs by his providence, which reaches from one end of the earth to the other and orders all things well."[8] In our times, temperance becomes the celebration of life, of its gift to us by God. Within an ecological stance of care for all of creation, temperance is not a human act of self-discipline; it is an act in harmony with the living presence of God within us.

Conclusion

Concentration and focus are necessary to accomplish any difficult or time-consuming task. By looking at the fundamental characteristics of a spiritual life, we see patterns that have developed over the centuries for Christians who choose to live fully human lives, lives in which the will governs the body. Temperance is self-discipline. Our ability to focus both body and mind means that we can craft a life that is intentional and purposefully Christian. However, a life of spiritual self-discipline is not the summit of the spiritual life, for that is worship, in which we place ourselves in God's presence. Spiritual self-discipline has not always been fruitful, but at its best, it unites us with the divine presence of God and lets us celebrate the gift of life.

Chapter Seven

FORTITUDE

Now the eleven disciples went to Galilee, to the mountain to which Jesus had directed them. And when they saw him they worshiped him; but some doubted. And Jesus came and said to them, "All authority in heaven and on earth has been given to me. Go therefore and make disciples of all nations, baptizing them in the name of the Father and of the Son and of the Holy Spirit, teaching them to observe all that I have commanded you; and lo, I am with you always, to the close of the age." —Matthew 28:16–20

Now fortitude above all lays claim to praise for steadfastness. Because he that stands firm is so much the more praised, as he is more strongly impelled to fall or recede....And among the pains of the mind and dangers those are mostly feared which lead to death, and it is against them that the brave man stands firm. Therefore fortitude is a cardinal virtue.

—St. Thomas Aquinas, *Summa Theologica,*—II-II, Q. 123, art. 11.

◆ ◆ ◆

A T THE HEART of Aristotle's reasoning was his interest in the courage of the warrior. For Aristotle, right conduct in war was neither cowardly nor foolhardy; rather it stood between the two. The "in between" was courage. For most people today, the battle seems to be between courage and fear. We fear failure. We won't try because we imagine ourselves losing, and find that unacceptable. We fear rejection. We try to love and find friends but are afraid we will not be accepted and loved. We fear what people will think. We try to live up to the expectations of others, even when they make us conform to disvalues.

In the face of real failure, rejection, and insult, it is possible to persevere, to make it to a better place, a better time. But the ability to face and live through suffering calls upon us to find and rely on an inner strength. That strength is fortitude.

Who Has Courage?

It was the first weekend of summer. The weather was warm, the river inviting. Grieving over the loss of their mother and wife, this small family, fishing poles and lunch in hand, headed out to play, to laugh, to live and enjoy the day with their friends. A father, two six-year-old twin boys, and Helen, a family friend, stood on the muddy riverbank. It was the last weekend of May, the water still cold and the underwater currents fast and strong. Billy slips and falls into the river. Almost in an instant, he's pulled under the water and bobs downstream. Screaming, scrambling, people run back and forth along the bank. Eddie, his father, jumps into the water. Helen follows him. Both are pulled along in the strong currents. Eddie grabs Billy, and lifts him over his head. Pushed down river, they float toward a pier. Quick hands grab Billy. Eddie has lost consciousness and slips under the water. John Hanson, one of their friends, jumps in and grabs him. With the help of others on the pier, Eddie and Helen are pulled from the water. Eddie's not breathing. Mr. Hanson begins CPR. The paramedics arrive, but it's too late. They can't revive him. Eddie is dead. Helen is taken to the hospital in critical condition.

Not with idle curiosity but sincere sympathy, news of these events spreads throughout the community. The local newspaper reports the story and interviews family and neighbors. "What parent wouldn't risk their own life for the life of their child? There's no thought behind that action. He cared for them very much, and he did what he could to provide them a good life. Like any parent, he did what he had to do."[1] Who has courage? A dad. A friend.

The extraordinary thing about courage is that it is not so extraordinary. People do heroic things every day. The practice of this virtue for Christians, then, is both conceivable and possible. What would be the path for Christians to develop the strength and purpose to overcome their fears and face whatever risks were placed before them, to do what needs to be done?

Theological Reflection

In the chapter on temperance we discussed the nature of a spiritual life and the place of prayer in that life. The psalms of the Old Testament were mentioned as central to the life of the monasteries. The psalms richly express the faith of Israel, and Christians carried them into their sacred texts, because they also spoke to their faith in God. Praise, lament, gratitude, longing, loneliness, and fear are expressed in the psalms, as well as joy, vindication, confidence, and renewed faith. The intensity of union with God, the depths of despair, the fear of death and suffering, the comfort of the peace of forgiveness and reconciliation — the gamut of human experience is expressed in the poetry of the psalms. Perhaps they remain central to Jewish and Christian prayer because their richness is never exhausted.

When we think about courage, and the road to find it, praying the psalms makes perfect sense: "My strength and courage is the Lord, and he has been my savior" (Psalm 118). One commentator wrote to introduce the psalm, "On the day of distress, when all other hope fails, it is God who is strength and safety, light and blessing."[2] I remember Beverly, a woman of eighty-nine who was admitted to our special hospice home, built by the hospital but freestanding and family-friendly. She was near the end of her life and was tended carefully by her children and grandchildren. I visited her each day, as one of my responsibilities as chaplain. The first day I met her, Beverly handed me a small card, well-worn and crumpled. On it was printed the Twenty-Third Psalm:

The Lord is my shepherd;
I shall not want.
In verdant pastures he gives me repose;
beside restful waters he leads me;
he refreshes my soul.

He guides me in right paths for his name's sake.
Even though I walk in the dark valley I fear no evil;
for you are at my side
with your rod and your staff that give me courage.

She asked me to pray with her and read the psalm, which is what I did each day. And I could see the comfort it gave her, the peacefulness with which she approached her death. She did not fear death, for God was with her, a shepherd guiding and protecting her. Trusting in God is the foundation of fortitude.

The example of Jesus is the foundation for a Christian understanding of courage. The events surrounding his arrest and death are recorded in the Gospels. They tell the story of the last time he gathered with his followers. They shared a meal together in a small room in Jerusalem and then left the city and walked up a hill to a grove of olive trees. There Jesus told his disciples to wait while he prayed: "Abba, Father, all things are possible to you. Take this cup away from me, but not what I will but what you will" (Mark 14:36). Everything was about to change, and the path ahead was full of pain and suffering. Jesus, the divine incarnate son of God, had to prepare himself to endure what lay ahead. And the whole story of Christianity exists because Jesus had the courage to say "yes" to God's will.

Courage in Our Times

A generation is slowly passing away, one that lived through terrible times: the Great Depression, the rise of Nazism, Hitler's campaign to exterminate the Jews and in league with Mussolini to conquer Europe, the bombing of Pearl Harbor, the battles in the Pacific, the finding of the bodies and survivors in the death camps, the nuclear bombs dropped on Nagasaki and Hiroshima. The men and women who lived through these experiences were marked indelibly by them. And their children and grandchildren were left to cope with their aftermath. In these dark times, there were many acts of courage, some heralded in the history books, some remembered by family, and some carried to the grave in anonymity.

Of the figures that emerged in this era, Sir Winston Churchill looms large. His leadership and pivotal role in the defeat of Adolf Hitler have been well chronicled. In his memoirs, Churchill writes about his speech before the British Parliament on June 4, 1940, after the evacuation from Dunkirk "to explain not only to our own people but to the world that our resolve to fight on was based on serious grounds, and was no mere despairing effort. It was also right to lay bare my own reasons for confidence."[3] This speech was decisive in securing the help of the United States. His argument was simply this, that no matter what happened, Britain would never give up.

> Even though large tracts of Europe and many old and famous States have fallen or may fall into the grip of the Gestapo and all the odious apparatus of Nazi rule, we shall not flag or fail. We shall go on to the end, we shall fight in France, we shall fight in the seas and oceans, we shall fight with growing confidence and growing strength in the air, we shall defend our island, whatever the cost may be, we shall fight on

the beaches, we shall fight on the landing-grounds, we shall fight in the fields and in the streets, we shall fight in the hills; we shall never surrender, and even if, which I do not for a moment believe, this island or a large part of it were subjugated and starving, then our Empire beyond the seas, armed and guarded by the British Fleet, would carry on the struggle, until, in God's good time, the New World, with all its power and might, steps forth to the rescue and the liberation of the Old.[4]

The people of Britain would never acquiesce. That truth gave them courage because they had the power to sustain hope, regardless of the day-to-day circumstances militating against it. For hope rested on their own resolve, and nothing else.

Courage in the dire circumstances of war impressed Aristotle. It was the motivation for his study of the virtues. Courage comes in many forms and is played out in many circumstances. For people in the United States whose lives continue to be affected by the attacks of September 11, 2001, people's heroism is remembered and celebrated. So many stories are told of that terrible day. Two I think of now. There was a man who died in the Twin Towers because he would not abandon his friend who was wheelchair bound and could not escape down the stairs. "Go on without me." But he would not. They stayed together and died together. The morning after 9/11 a man found his wife out in their yard planting tulip bulbs, confident that spring would come and the bulbs would bloom. So many people were terrified, sure that the world was coming to an end.

But she was planting tulip bulbs to say that she believed in the future. Courage is never giving up.

"Courage Is a Verb; Do It"[5]

To understand courage in our own times we need to explore it from different angles, to spend time together thinking it through. Other voices should come into play. Katherine Platt, associate professor of cultural anthropology at Babson College, wrote a simple primer, an instructional manual in five steps, on how one learns to act courageously:

> I argue that if we were to dissect an episode of courageous action, we would find a combination of the following preexisting mental and spiritual labors (although not necessarily in this order) making the courageous action possible: inner honesty, consciousness of choice, vision of the courageous action, intention, decision to act.[6]

On the path of her reflections, Dr. Platt wants to know what courage is, for a reason. She wants to see what it takes for people to be courageous. The model she created makes courage accessible. To be courageous is a choice, based on rational thought and a personal commitment. And courage is not a personality trait; it is an action. If we take seriously the notion that courage is a virtue, that it is an acquired habit, then it seems reasonable that with practice people can transform insecurity, doubt, and fear into acts of integrity.

Courage as Leadership

Courage is neither foolhardiness nor cowardice. Courage is a calculated risk, a decision, a willingness to take risks for a greater good. In our times, what would Christian courage be? Looking at the last encounter of Jesus with his followers, when they are gathered on the mountain in Galilee, we see what the earliest Christians faced. After the agony of Jesus' death on the cross and the amazing events of his resurrection, the disciples come to discover that this is the end of the road. Jesus is leaving. The passage in Matthew shows that the confidence of some of them was so shaky that they had not even grasped the reality of the resurrection. And instead of a joyous reunion, they were faced with separation. They were to assume responsibility for Jesus' ministry, preaching and healing, sharing the good news of salvation. They were to assume the authority that went with that ministry. And although Jesus promised that he would be with them, it was their responsibility to bear these burdens. From our vantage point in history, we see the suffering that was entailed. Many of Jesus' followers met with persecution, torture, and death. They were called cannibals by the Roman authorities for their weird practices in the catacombs. The courage of leadership marks the life of a Christian. Being a leader may very well mean suffering for those you serve, but that is a choice that people have made for hundreds of years. It is why, in fact, Christianity exists.

Conclusion

As St. Thomas Aquinas states, fortitude lays claim to stead-fastness. The ability to be faithful, to your friends, your family, your beliefs, your standards, your values, to do what needs to be done to protect them, is the virtue of courage. If writing a dissertation is a test of character, per-haps we could say that ultimately, the way you live your life is a test of character. To be courageous is to act coura-geously in situations where it matters. To be courageous is to persevere.

For Christians, the challenge of leadership was not a burden without its graces. The followers of Jesus had each other. Jesus formed a community and worked hard to bring them together to support and care for one another. And so we continue to do today.

Part Three

Choosing Life
in Community

Chapter Eight

COMMUNION

And all who believed were together and had all things in common; and they sold their possessions and goods and distributed them to all, as any had need. And day by day, attending the temple together and breaking bread in their homes, they partook of food with glad and generous hearts, praising God and having favor with all the people.

—Acts 2:44–47

◆ ◆ ◆

LIVING A VIRTUOUS LIFE, what ultimately does it mean? Why expend the effort to perfect one's character, even at the price of sacrifice and diminishment? Our last chapter focused on the why of it all: Why live a virtuous life? The goal of the virtuous life is communion, with God and with our families, friends, and neighbors, with our ancestors and the human race, the planet and all its living things, the stars in the universe. Being virtuous is simply opening a door to a deeper life that unites us with the life around us. A truly human life centers both on the divine presence within and around us, beyond us in its fullness and perfection, and the community that accompanies us on this journey called life. Communion is expressed in many ways and has always been central to religious life.

Communion with God

We begin our reflections by considering the nature of communion with God. The Christian community has felt invited into a relationship with God through God's self-gift. We attempt to relate to God, because human beings feel drawn by something. Returning to Joachim Wach's notion of genuine religious experience, we can say that human beings from generation to generation have encountered the divine presence of God and have moved toward it with humility and awe.[1] This awareness of the sacred leads human beings to a response of devotion and service. Devotion becomes the ritualized response to ultimate reality.

> Because a person is not made of pure mind or spirit, material forms (images, sounds, gestures, rites, guilds, organizations) are necessary.... It has been rightly stated that these forms objectify what otherwise might remain as subjective and individual aspirations; and that they render concrete — as well as channel — the graces from above.[2]

And service denotes that deepening understanding of God's love for the universe, for all living things and for every human being.

> In confronting Ultimate Reality man realizes the obligation which his true nature — understood in terms of this confrontation — imposes upon him.... In Christianity the aim is to be filled with the spirit of God and to obey the divine word in full communion with the living Christ, to anticipate life in the kingdom

which is redemption from sin and guilt, and to hope for forgiveness and for the peace which passes all understanding.[3]

That sense of imposition, moral and spiritual, comes in the form of loyal duty, to serve God by caring for the world that God has created. Christian mystics, imbued with a deep sense of the holy presence of God, speak of their love for all of humanity, indeed for all living things. But according to Wach, the religious expressions of this divine encounter are most completely embodied by a community; "the common acts of devotion and service provide an incomparable bond of union between the members of a cult-group. Praying together is the token of the deepest spiritual communion. To join in a specific act of devotion may constitute a permanent association."[4]

Characteristics of the Rituals of Devotion

Exploring the rituals and prayers of worship, we begin by situating worship in time and space. When we think about time and liturgy, two categories come into play, "sacred time" and "ordinary time." They are distinct and separate entities, yet intermingled. The notion of sacred time invites us to consider God's presence in ordinary life, the in-breaking of the divine into human existence. According to our understanding of salvation history God invites humanity into relationship and then works through history to offer healing, grace, and salvation. The Scriptures are often described as the story of salvation history, where the dream of the eschaton, the transformation of all of life in accord with God's eternal plan, inspires the lives of believers from generation to generation. Christians hold that God's plan for the human race is revealed in the events of Jesus' life, death, and resurrection. When Catholics gather to pray and celebrate the liturgy, there is a sense that sacred time joins with ordinary time, that eternity touches historical progression, and the kingdom has begun. Within the context of worship, past events are recalled and made present for the community gathered, creating a sense of the fluidity of time, as past, present, and future come together and sacred time is made present in ordinary time.

Ordinary time is a familiar concept and experience. We live in time, and can see the passage of time in our own lives: once we were children, and now we are adults. Ordinary time can reveal the sacred, however, and many Catholic theologians would argue that the sacraments are a bridge between the ordinary and the sacred. Significant experiences in so-called ordinary life, such as the birth of a child, are so filled with the mystery and holiness of God that they rightly enter sacred time.

James White points out that the life of the Christian community depends heavily on the structures of ordinary time, the days of the week, the seasons of the year.[5] Christian worship has "times" and "seasons" and celebrates the events in Jesus' life, as well as the lives of the saints, in its yearly calendar. The most ordinary use of time in everyday life, White noted, also reveals our priorities. "Spending time with the Lord" is a statement used in traditional spiritual direction, marking the value of making oneself available for prayer.

To understand the nature of worship, it's necessary to consider the power and place of time, as it defines and expands the encounter with God that occurs. Within a liturgical gathering, ordinary time is drawn into the eternal, and simple actions take on mythic proportions.

Sacred Space

"Sacred space" suggests the unique nature of the gathering place for worship. Sacred space begins with the concept of sacred places. Ancient cultures marked the existence of sacred places, filled with the spiritual presence of God or the ancestors. Even in the rush of modern life, many people find peace when they gaze on an ocean or up to the top of a mountain. The notion, then, of a place being able to contain something spiritual is within our realm of understanding, perhaps forming part of our symbolic imaginations. Some point to evidence that the early Christian churches built in Ireland were located on sites already considered holy by the people, thus assimilating and transforming the community's sense of the sacred.

The Christian community's gathering places for prayer in the early church were homes, and later Roman basilicas. But holy sites in Jerusalem, such as the place where Jesus was crucified, were immortalized with the building of churches. Holy sites were marked and later simply created by bringing the remains of saints and martyrs to be buried within the boundaries of the church.

Churches to the present day are created purposefully as places where one can go to encounter the divine. Church architecture, the structure of the building, its grandeur or intimacy, the use of space, light, and color, the placement of art and sculpture, the nature of the worship and rituals that take place in the space reveal the ways in which people experience the presence of God in their lives and their prayer, and the way the space mediates, supports, and enables that experience. Abbot Suger (AD 1081–1150) of the royal abbey of St. Denis in Paris recognized a deep symbolic value to the use of light in the construction of a church. Lawrence Cunningham has written:

> While Suger's architectural work was under way, he wrote two small booklets, *On Administration* and *On the Consecration of a Church.* They are goldmines of information on the ideas that stand behind Suger's architectural work. Underlying Suger's whole plan of construction and decoration was the theology of beauty based on the mysticism of light. Suger was heavily influenced by his reading of Pseudo-Dionysius . . . [who] believed that every created thing partakes, however imperfectly, in the essence of God. There is an ascending hierarchy of existence that ranges from the grossness of matter to the purity of light. The ultimate light, of course, is God. Everything that is perceived is perceived in the light of its creator, which is God. As light becomes more pure (i.e., as we leave the grossness of matter), we get closer to God. Suger applied these ideas to his church building. His desire was for people to come in from the profane space of the world and be bathed in a sea of light. This light-filled building would be conceived as a sort of foretaste of God's light in heaven.[6]

Art and Music

In the case of a church like St. Denis, sacred space is carefully crafted, as natural light is coaxed through stained-glass windows. *Sacred art, sculpture,* and *paintings,* are other ways in which churches create sacred space. They express the story of Christianity visually and foster prayer and meditation. In the Eastern Christian tradition, icons elevate the union of art and prayer, creating a window to the sacred that is quite unique.[7] Images of Jesus, his childhood, ministry, his suffering and death, form a large part of the art usually present in Catholic churches. The body of Jesus on the cross is a common image, as are the Stations of the Cross, a meditative collection of images that follow the path of the passion of Jesus, his arrest, torture, and death. But Mary the mother of Jesus, the saints, and the martyrs have also been carved on the walls and exterior doors, as well as painted as frescoes. The story of Christianity, a religion rooted in the history of people, ordinary and holy, seems naturally to be expressed through the stories of people, through images depicting events in their lives.

Sometimes, unfortunately, space can fail to serve a community's prayer needs. And so the question of the nature of sacred space, and whether it is possible to create a special place to enter the holy, remains important to ministers and believing communities. Of course, sacred space is really about the people gathered to pray to God. The gathering of a worshiping community is what makes space sacred. Brian Doyle, the editor of *Portland* magazine at the University of Portland, Oregon, wrote about his experiences one Sunday morning.

A little Catholic university chapel, all cedar and sunlight, amid a riot of rhododendrons. Behind the chapel a crowd of muscular old oak trees. Before it a sea of fresh-cut grass, dotted with scrawny cherry trees, toddlers, dandelions. Above it a ragged arrowhead of geese, southing.... Mass begins, gently. ... "This morning we gather as a faith community to broaden our vision," says the young priest. He will utter the word "community" seven times this morning, by my count; tribal binding is the clear theme of this Mass. Two other priests are robed and on the altar, and the whole crowd sings lustily, holds hands while chanting the Our Father, exchanges hearty handshakes of peace at startling length (one energetic boy making his way completely around the chapel). All but a handful will receive Communion; all but a handful will stay after Mass to chat in cheerful knots; all, apparently, are excited and stimulated by Mass. This crowd isn't dutiful; it's pumped. Rumors of death of faith among youth greatly exaggerated, at least this morning.[8]

And the whole crowd sings lustily. When we begin to consider the notion of "sounds" we need to think about language and verbal expression, voice and instrument, sound and silence. The ability of human beings to move language into song is fundamentally obvious, and yet participates in the wonder and complexity of the human brain. Music is natural to the human race and preexists any Christian expression. In fact, to use or not to use music and song can be traced to debates and problems that move throughout the history of Christianity.

There is a long and rich history of the use of music and song in Christian worship. Chant, monastic rhythms of praying the psalms, were a highlight of the Middle Ages. The almost revolutionary developments in music that arose from Martin Luther's imagination during the Reformation mark another distinct development in Christian music. James White points to the works of Johann Sebastian Bach and their contribution to Lutheran worship. John and Charles Wesley were eighteenth-century Methodists in England. "In 1745, the Wesleys published *Hymns on the Lord's Supper,* which still remains the greatest treasury of eucharistic hymns in English. When one studies it, one soon recognizes that much of it comes from a theological treatise on the Eucharist by Daniel Brevint. The Wesleys turned the treatise into poetry. The Wesleys' converts both sang and learned their new faith."[9] Musical expression is natural to the human person, and so it naturally flows into worship.

Ritual

Once the stage is set, sacred space created and maintained, sacred time is initiated as the ritual begins. What is a religious ritual? It's a sacred drama, the most important play of life. Across the world's religions, it may change in form and content, but it expresses the deepest meanings and longings of the people gathered. It begins in ordinary time and opens the community to the eternal presence of the Sacred—ultimate reality as it is conceived. The drama of life is played out across time and space, communicated in stories, poetry, music and song, dance and touch, gestures of respect, blessing, humility. Candles are lit, incense is burned, flowers arranged for beauty. Catholic rituals incorporate all of the senses and span the full life cycle from birth to death.

Back in the third century, Hippolytus recorded the early rituals of Christianity in Rome. The rite of baptism marked the religious birth of individuals as they committed themselves to the Christian faith and way of life.

Then, after these things, let him give over to the presbyter, who baptizes, and let the candidates stand in the water, naked, a deacon going with them likewise. And when he who is being baptized goes down into the water, he who baptizes him, putting his hand on him, shall say thus: "Dost thou believe in God, the Father Almighty?" And he who is baptized shall say: "I believe."

Then, holding his hand placed on his head he shall baptize him once and then he shall say: "Dost thou believe in Christ Jesus, the Son of God, who was born of the Holy Ghost of the Virgin Mary, and was crucified under Pontius Pilate, and was dead and buried, and rose again the third day, alive from the dead, and ascended into heaven, and sat at the right hand of the Father, and will come to judge the quick and the dead?"

And when he says, "I believe," he is baptized again. And again he shall say: "Dost thou believe in the Holy

Ghost and the holy church and the resurrection of the flesh?"

He who is being baptized shall say accordingly: "I believe," and so is baptized a third time.

And afterward, when he has come up [out of the water], he is anointed by the presbyter with the oil of thanksgiving, the presbyter saying: "I anoint thee with holy oil in the name of Jesus Christ." And so each one, after drying himself, is immediately clothed, and then is brought into the church.[10]

A spiritual director once told me that "your strength is your weakness." The strongest characteristics of your personality, which mark your identity and on which you depend, bring their own costs, cause their own difficulties. And here is a similar example. For many people today, Christianity as a historical religion poses problems. A religion based on revelation, on the existence of a man named Jesus who united the divine and human within him, who walked the earth in Israel two thousand years ago, is more problematic than a purely philosophical or independently spiritual set of beliefs. And yet there is something strongly comforting about the historical character of Christianity. For here a ritual of the third century has been preserved from the past as record and continues to be celebrated today. The words of baptism and the sprinkling of water occur today, in churches on Sunday with proud moms and dads and godparents holding the usually squirmy baby, and in the Easter mysteries at the Easter vigil, where adults step forward with their sponsors and make the same baptismal vows as the Christians in Rome did in AD 215.

Sacraments

Within the Catholic heritage the primary rituals are called sacraments. We first discussed sacraments in the chapter on faith, stating that these rituals celebrate life and open the human family to God's presence. These sacraments open the ordinary stages of life—birth, adulthood, marriage, old age, and dying — to be consciously lived out in the presence of God. These combine the ordinary and the divine, ordinary time and eternity. For the Catholic Church, the fundamental meaning of the sacraments was solidified in the teachings of the Council of Trent, at which the bishops tried to recover the church's direction after the challenges of the Protestant Reformation in the sixteenth century. The sacraments conferred grace.[11] In chapter 2 on hope we talked about God's goodness sustaining all of life and the empowerment of human beings by grace to face evil. We are bathed in the light of grace, and through that experience of grace we are empowered. Catholics have held on to the centrality of their religious celebrations, believing that the rituals called sacraments sustain us for the journey of life. In the language and imagery of the sixteenth-century church, the sacraments are necessary for salvation. To finish the journey of life well and find eternal happiness, we need the presence of the Christian community in our lives.

At the heart of that community's presence is the Sunday gathering and the celebration of the *Eucharist*. At the Last Supper, Jesus took bread and wine and, giving thanks to God, he broke the bread and gave it to his disciples and told them to take and eat it, for it was his body. He gave them the cup and told them to take and drink it for it was his blood, poured out for their salvation. And then he told them to do this again, in his memory. The mystery of this ritual was born the night Jesus was arrested. Over all the centuries since that time, in many corners of the world, Christians have gathered and remembered Jesus with these words and actions. There has been no small amount of controversy in this matter — from Romans thinking Christians were cannibals to bitter debates in the sixteenth century and the severance of ties among Christians over the theological import of Jesus' words and actions. In the modern era, especially through the work of the World Council of Churches, we are experiencing renewed hope for reconciliation. The theological concept of *real presence* has emerged as a possible point of intersection among the Christian churches that can agree that Jesus is present when the words of institution are said and the Holy Spirit is invoked. For Catholics, the celebration of the Eucharist is the full expression of union of body and spirit with the risen Christ.

Our Lady of Guadalupe

Catholic rituals include not only the sacraments, but also special devotions and sacramentals. Central to modern Catholic prayer and ritual is devotion to Jesus' mother, Mary. The creation in the eleventh century of the set of prayers now known as the Rosary marks the centralization and cohesion of a long tradition of devotion to Mary. Belief in the *communion of saints* is a fundamental stance taken by Catholics, who affirm that the beloved dead are not fully removed and indifferent to the fate of people on earth. Ours is a community of the living and the dead. Our lost loved ones, a parent, a child, are never forgotten, nor have they lost their place in our lives. They live, in our memories, our hearts, and our minds. We think of them, talk to them. For Christians who believe in life after death, they live on in eternity. Mary lives on in eternity, and her goodness shelters us.

In 1521 outside of Mexico City our Lady appeared to Juan Diego, a member of an Indian community oppressed by the occupying Spanish conquistadors. "Let not your heart be disturbed," she said. "Am I not here? Who is your Mother? Are you not under my protection? Am I not your health? Are you not happily within my fold? What else do you wish? Do not grieve nor be disturbed by anything."[12] The experience of Mary's love and protection in a time of terrible need set the stage for life-changing events in Mexico and to this day has sustained devotions within the Hispanic communities. Devotion to Our Lady of Guadalupe has strongly influenced the broader expressions of Catholicism around the world.

The World at Prayer

"Hear, O Israel, the Lord is Our God, the Lord is One," is the first line of the *Shema*, from Deuteronomy 6:7, a prayer to be said in the morning and at night by observant Jews.[13] The mystery of God's presence in the world and the human desire to draw near that presence invites us to consider the many ways in which humanity worships that ultimate reality. In solidarity with our ancient roots in Judaism, Christians find much in common with the patterns of worship of Judaism. The present-day practice of *Shabbat,* for example, a day set aside for the Lord, has much to commend itself in a world of harried lives.[14]

The call to prayer for Muslims, *Allahu Akbar,* "God is Great," repeated four times, and then *Laa elaaha Ella Allah,* "There is no god besides God," draws the attention of the community five times during the day, beginning at dawn and ending at night prayer.[15] I visited a Muslim community in the Southwest that sponsored a summer program of Islamic studies for teachers. Their hospitality was extraordinary, and their efforts to build bridges of understanding between cultures and religions were a powerful witness to their faith in God. Sharing prayer with the community, I was deeply moved by how central their prayer life was to their very existence. Perhaps Catholicism has differentiated its roles too much, delegating intense prayer to vowed religious while laypeople attend to their families, jobs, and communities. The model of the Muslim family at prayer spoke volumes about the choices that had been made and the priorities that had been emphasized.

Sacred spaces are central to Christian worship, and the rituals that surround the altar are essential in the liturgical celebrations of Eastern Christianity. But the use of an altar is not unique to Christians. In the practice of Buddhism, creating a home altar is an important religious expression.[16] Incense, candles, statues, and pictures are arranged according to tradition. Although there is some disagreement over the extent to which material things are needed for prayer, it is understandable that human beings, whose lives are intertwined with the natural world, would incorporate that world into whatever they do. And it certainly is clear that Catholics can find much in common with their sisters and brothers around the world in their efforts to be in the presence of the Sacred.

Conclusion

I set before you life and death, the blessing and the curse.
Choose life.   —Deuteronomy 30:19, Moses to the people of Israel

Why live the virtuous life? We have explored the way in which virtue brings communion with God and others. We have seen the importance of the solidarity of community and the function of worship in guiding our understanding of God's presence in our lives. The virtuous life is not lived alone. It is lived in community. When Moses looks out over the promised land with the people of Israel, he challenges them to make a fundamental choice: to accept a life in harmony with God's will and receive its blessings, or to turn away from that path and suffer the emptiness of that loss. As their leader, he challenges them: "choose life." To live a Christian life of the virtues is just that, choosing life.

CONCLUSION

We call upon Christians, Jews, Muslims, and all believ-
ers in God.... Knowledge is the cure for one's ignorance.
"And you shall know the truth, and the truth shall make
you free" (The Bible, John 8:32). "You shall not accept any
information, unless you verify it yourself. I have given you
the hearing, the eyesight, and the brain, and you are re-
sponsible for using them" (The Quran, 17:36).... The time
has now come that we can not remain silent.... We hope
to bring love, peace, and tolerance into this world based
on respect, compassion, and a solid foundation of knowl-
edge. May God bless all who strive for peace and true
happiness.[1]   —One Muslim community

The Legitimacy of Religious Experience

How can we legitimately identify, describe, and justify experiences that make claims of some kind of connection
with ultimate reality?[2] Unfortunately, it seems that we are
in the same place as Pontius Pilate asking, "What is truth?"
(John 18:38). In the name of religion individuals will strap
a bomb onto their body, walk into a restaurant crowded
with families, and explode the bomb, killing themselves
and anyone within range.[3] And yet truth-claims are made,

143

and people's lives are lived out within the constructs of religious belief and ethical norms. Is there a path to solid ground when we talk about religious experience?

Years ago when I was pursuing my master's degree at Catholic Theological Union, I took a graduate course in contextual theology taught by Stephen Bevans, S.V.D. His strategy was to explore the way in which theology balanced the complex network of language, race, culture, ethnicity, historical experience, religious experience, and spirituality. He proposed a methodology for what he termed "contextual theology," which I believe would be a useful tool for sorting through the many issues raised in this text on virtue. Bevans points to an avenue for constructing truth in a world, as defined by David Tracy, filled with "plurality and ambiguity."[4]

> Truth will not be reached by one point of view trying to convince all the others that it alone is correct. That is neither possible, nor, as the situation has revealed, even desirable. It was possible in a world that saw truth as a simple correspondence between concept and reality; but the same world was one that also prescribed one culture and one way of thinking for all. It was, as Shorter calls it, a worldview of "monoculturalism." Contemporary postmodern thinking, however, is moving away from this correspondence understanding of truth and understanding truth more in terms of relation, conversation, and dialogue. Truth, in this scheme of things, is understood not so much as something "out there," but as a reality that emerges

in true conversation between authentic men and women when they "allow questioning to take over."[5]

Authentic Existence

The primacy of experience for our cognitive and moral development is central to human existence in the twenty-first century, and that will not go away. The notion of a plurality of experiences and of truths is a path that opens up the best possibility of making sense of religious experience and its legitimacy. And hand in hand with that plurality go its partners, dialogue and accountability. The truth of one person's experience stands next to the truth of another person's, and in community we come to see the potential value for shared experience and truth. And if Bevans is right that we do not possess universal truths, then it seems possible to be concrete and specific to the present moment.

The notion of "authentic women and men" connects with Maurice Blondel's fundamental insight, in his book *L'Action* (1893), that all people are forced to act, to make decisions with enormous consequences, and to live with them, regardless of whether we have come to know and own some kind of truth. We can't stop living to wait for answers. Perhaps then we could say that authentic existence is one that is fully engaged with the task of living, and Christian existence is one that is fully engaged with the task of living in relation to the person of Jesus, whom the Christian community came to experience as the risen Lord. Authentic women and men are the dialogue partners in fashioning norms for legitimate religious experience. We can also say that claims to genuine religious experience will not go away. Religion is structured on the premise that there is ultimate reality and that human beings experience that reality. The modern world has not stripped human experience of its sense of the infinite, nor has Christianity diverted from its path of two thousand years of faith in a God who saves. Turning to tradition is part of our self-understanding as historical beings, whose present exists within the context of past and future.

In exploring the life of Christian virtue, we can stand with others on their own journeys and in our troubled times find authentic women and men who will choose life with us.

NOTES

Introduction

1. Karl Rahner, a twentieth-century Jesuit priest and theologian, centered his philosophical and theological discussions on this question.

2. Aristotle, *Nicomachean Ethics,* in *The Basic Works of Aristotle,* ed. Richard McKeon (New York: Random House, 1941), Bk. II, chap. 5.

3. Aquinas, *Introduction to Saint Thomas Aquinas,* ed. Anton C. Pegis (New York: Random House, 1945), ST I, 61, 1. Thomas points to Ambrose's reflections on Luke 6:20: "blessed are the poor in spirit." St. Ambrose lived from AD 304 to 397. "Although still a catechumen, he was persuaded by the bishops, the clergy, and the people to let himself be baptized, ordained, and consecrated at the age of thirty-four. As archbishop of Milan, he became a successful teacher and an eloquent preacher, opposed the Arians successfully, and resisted all attempts of the civil power to interfere in Church affairs." See Joseph McSorley, *An Outline History of the Church by Centuries* (St. Louis: Herder, 1943), 92.

4. Joachim Wach, *The Comparative Study of Religions* (New York: Columbia University Press, 1958).

Chapter 1: Faith

1. The image of "diving into darkness" emerged when I was working on a paper on the nature of religious experience for a conference. It's a powerful image, and emblematic of the depth of risk that faith entails.

2. Roger Aubert, *Le Probleme de l'Act de foi* (Louvain: Editions Nauwelaerts, 1969).

3. Lawrence S. Cunningham, *The Catholic Heritage* (New York: Crossroad, 1989): "God is known to us through nature, the unfolding of history, the social reality of institutions, the goodness and the holiness of others, the power and efficacy of the church's sacramental life, and the preaching of God's word.... The reality of God is mediated through community" (30). Cunningham's insights help us to bridge what seems to be the vast divide between the time of the Pentecost and ordinary life today.

4. See Plato's *Republic.* The intellectual climate of Greco-Roman culture strongly influenced the theological development of Christianity. Understandably, the wealth of human reflection on life became a basis for interpreting the new experience of the early Christians. Diogenes Allen observes: "For Plato, as for Christianity, this world is not our home. We have a destiny which cannot be fully achieved here, and human life is a journey from this world to ultimate reality. Plato and Christianity differ on the nature of this world, on what our true home is, and on how we get there. But their common insistence that the sensible world depends on a nonsensible reality and that our happiness or well-being is to be found there makes them allies. Plato provided great support for Christianity against materialist views in the ancient world. Augustine in his *Confessions* describes the assistance he received from the Platonists. He said that they enabled him to overcome in his journey to Christianity the hindrance caused by his own inability to conceive of any reality that was not sensible" (*Philosophy for Understanding Theology* [Atlanta: John Knox, 1969], 39).

5. The hindsight of modern historians reads the confrontation between Pope Urban VIII and Galileo as a drama of personalities rather than of scientific theories. See "The Dispute between Galileo and the Catholic Church Parts 1 & 2," by Donald Demarco at *www.catholiceducation.org.*

6. *Decrees of Vatican Ecumenical Council I,* Session 3, Chap. 4, *www.intratext.com/ixt/eng0063/_p8.htm.*

7. John Paul II, *Fides et Ratio, www.vatican.va/holy_father/john_paul_ii/encyclicals/documents/hf_jp-ii_enc_15101.*

8. Ibid., no. 30.

9. John F. Haught, *God after Darwin: A Theology of Evolution* (Boulder, Colo.: Westview Press, 2000).

10. Ibid., 81.

11. Erik Erikson, *Childhood and Society* (New York: Norton, 1950). The eight stages identified by Erikson are Basic Trust vs. Basic Mistrust, Autonomy vs. Shame, Initiative vs. Guilt, Industry vs. Inferiority, Identity vs. Identity Diffusion, Intimacy vs. Isolation, Generativity vs. Self-Absorption, Integrity vs. Despair.

Chapter 2: Hope

1. Of course, Christianity is not the only religious tradition whose members have such experiences.

2. See the 1971 Peck and Schrut study, quoted by Allan Schwartz, in "The Epidemiology of Suicide among Students at Colleges and Universities in the United States," *College Student Suicide,* ed. Leighton C. Whitaker and Richard E. Slimak (New York: Haworth, 1990), 38.

3. Edwin S. Shneidman, Ph.D., "Some Reflections of a Founder," in *Understanding and Preventing Suicide* (New York: Guilford Press, 1988), 6–8.

4. Milton Foreman, associate vice provost for health and psychological services at the University of Cincinnati, recommends assembling the social network of a student at risk. He suggests that the problems provoking the suicidal impulse are very often related to that network, and when those significant people are drawn into the intervention, it is effective. See Milton Foreman, "The Counselor's Assessment and Intervention with the Suicidal Student," in *College Student Suicide,* 125–40.

5. Martin Luther King Jr., "Acceptance Speech, on the occasion of the award of the Nobel Peace Prize, Oslo, December 10, 1964," *www.nobel.se/peace/laureates/1964/king-acceptance.html.*

6. The awakening of Catholic social teaching began much earlier, in the experience of the Industrial Revolution in Europe in the late nineteenth century and especially in the plight of factory workers. Pope Leo XIII's encyclical *Rerum Novarum* in 1891 articulated the Catholic position on the rights of the worker. When the Catholic

bishops met in the 1960s at the Second Vatican Council, their Pastoral Constitution on the Church in the Modern World expressed a vision of global solidarity.

7. Synod of Bishops Second General Assembly, *Justice in the World,* November 30, 1971, 74–76, in *The Gospel of Peace and Justice,* ed. Joseph Gremillion (Maryknoll, N.Y.: Orbis Books, 1976), 529.

8. See H. A. Guerber, *The Myths of Greece and Rome* (New York: American Book Co., 1907).

9. "The Legend of Prometheus and Pandora's Box," *www.physics .hku.k/~tboyce/ss/topics/prometheus.html.*

10. Ibid.

11. Joan D. Chittister, *Heart of Flesh: A Feminist Spirituality for Women and Men* (Ottawa: Novalis, 1998), 23.

12. Another conversation on suffering took place in Europe after the Holocaust, as theologians, philosophers, people of faith, and atheists struggled with their concepts of God in the face of the mass execution of millions of people in a supposedly Christian society. One of the leaders who emerged in this era of theology was Jürgen Moltmann, professor of systematic theology at the University of Tübingen. In his book *Theology of Hope* (New York: Harper & Row, 1967), he states: "To recognize the event of the resurrection of Christ is therefore to have a hopeful and expectant knowledge of this event. It means recognizing in this event the latency of that eternal life which in the praise of God arises from the negation of the negative, from the raising of the one who was crucified and the exaltation of the one who was forsaken. It means assenting to the tendency towards resurrection of the dead in this event of the raising of the one. It means following the intention of God by entering into the dialectic of suffering and dying in expectation of eternal life and of resurrection. This is described as the working of the Holy Spirit....The 'Spirit' in question here does not fall from heaven and does not soar ecstatically into heaven, but arises from the event of the resurrection of Christ and is an earnest and pledge of his future, of the future of universal resurrection and of life" (211).

13. James R. Brockman, *Romero: A Life* (Maryknoll, N.Y.: Orbis Books, 1990), 247–48. Archbishop Romero was shot and killed on March 24, 1980.

Chapter 3: Love

1. There are differences in interpretation of these categories. For example, C. S. Lewis identified these four as "affection, friendship, eros, and charity." See *The Four Loves* (New York: Harcourt, Brace & World, 1960).

2. I am indebted to my colleague at Duquesne University, Anne Clifford, for her reflections on the meaning of love, written in lecture notes for a course on theological anthropology, and especially for her insight into married love, which shows a level of respect and solidarity not consistently accorded throughout the history of the theology of marriage.

3. Richard of St. Victor, Book Three, Ch. VI, *Twelve Patriarchs, Mystical Ark, and Book Three of the Trinity,* trans. Grover Zinn (New York: Paulist, 1979), 379.

4. Maurice Blondel, *L'Action* (1893), trans. Oliva Blanchette (Notre Dame, Ind.: University of Notre Dame Press, 1985).

5. Mother Teresa, *Love: A Fruit Always in Season,* ed. Dorothy S. Hunt (San Francisco: Ignatius Press, 1987), 127.

6. The effects of abuse have been classified in the DSM-IV of the American Psychiatric Association as "post traumatic stress disorder."

7. Marie M. Fortune and James Poling, "Calling to Accountability: The Church's Response to Abusers," in *Violence against Women and Children,* ed. Carol J. Adams and Marie M. Fortune (New York: Continuum, 1998).

Chapter 4: Prudence

1. *Summa Theologica,* trans. Fathers of the English Dominican Province (Westminster, Md.: Christian Classics, 1920).

2. *Catechism of the Catholic Church* (Chicago: Loyola, 1994), n. 1806.

3. Elizabeth Johnson, *She Who Is* (New York: Crossroad, 1992).

4. Elisabeth Schüssler Fiorenza, *Jesus: Miriam's Child, Sophia's Prophet* (New York: Continuum, 1995), 136–37.

5. "Declaration on Religious Liberty," *Vatican Council II: The Conciliar and Post Conciliar Documents,* ed. Austin Flannery (New York: Costello, 1987), no. 2.

6. Ibid., no. 1.

7. John Henry Newman, *An Essay on the Development of Christian Doctrine* (New York: D. Appleton & Company, 1845), 19.

8. Karl Rahner, "Atheism and Implicit Christianity," *Theological Investigations,* vol. 9 (New York: Herder and Herder, 1972), 145–46.

9. Sr. Pascaline Coff, O.S.B., "Biography of Raimon Panikkar," on a website sponsored by North American Benedictine and Cistercian monasteries of men and women, *www.monasticdialog.com.*

10. Nirad C. Chaudhuri, *Hinduism* (New York: Oxford University Press, 1979), 147–48.

11. *The Bhagavad-Gita,* trans. Barbara Stoler Miller (New York: Bantam, 2004), the Sixth Teaching, 21–22, 68.

12. Seyyed Hossein Nasr, *The Heart of Islam: Enduring Values for Humanity* (San Francisco: HarperSanFrancisco, 2002), 43.

13. Emily Wax, "Islam Attracting Many Survivors of Rwanda Genocide," *Washington Post,* September 23, 2002.

14. The Dalai Lama, *The Way to Freedom* (San Francisco: HarperSanFrancisco, 1994), 155.

15. Mattie J. T. Stepanek, *Journey through Heartsongs* (New York: Hyperion, 2001), 54.

Chapter 5: Justice

1. Kathryn Tanner, "The Difference Theological Anthropology Makes," *Theology Today* 50, no. 4 (January 1994): 573–74. She points to Claus Westermann, *Creation* (Philadelphia: Fortress, 1971) and *Blessing in the Bible and the Life of the Church* (Philadelphia: Fortress, 1978); Jürgen Moltmann, *God in Creation: A New Theology of Creation and the Spirit of God* (San Francisco: HarperSanFrancisco, 1991); and James Barr, "Man and Nature," in *Ecology and Religion in History,* ed. David Spring and Eileen Spring (New York: Harper & Row, 1974), as

influencing her line of argument in interpreting "image of God" in this manner.

2. Cardinal Joseph Bernardin, "A Consistent Ethic of Life: An American-Catholic Dialogue," in *A Moral Vision for America,* ed. John Langan, S.J. (Washington, D.C.: Georgetown University Press, 1998), 14.

3. Bernardin, "The Catholic Moral Vision in the United States," in *A Moral Vision for America,* 157.

4. Eleanor Roosevelt, *The Great Question* (United Nations, 1958), quoted in Joseph P. Lash, *Eleanor: The Years Alone* (New York: W. W. Norton, 1972), 81.

Chapter 6: Temperance

1. Abbot Primate Jerome Theisen, O.S.B., notes in "The Rule of Saint Benedict: Introduction" that the Rule is built on the foundation of other monastic rules, including those of St. Pachomius (fourth-century Egypt), St. Basil (fourth-century Asia Minor), St. Augustine (fourth- and fifth-century North Africa), Cassian (fifth-century southern Gaul), and, the most important, the Rule of the Master (anonymous, fourth century). See *www.osb.org/gen/rule.html.*

2. The Dalai Lama, *Awakening the Mind, Lightening the Heart: Core Teachings of Tibetan Buddhism,* ed. Donald S. Lopez Jr. (San Francisco: HarperSanFrancisco, 1995), x–xi.

3. Seyyed Hossein Nasr, *The Heart of Islam: Enduring Values for Humanity* (San Francisco: HarperSanFrancisco, 2002), 133.

4. Rev. D. A. Donovan, O. Cist., *A Treatise of Spiritual Life,* trans. Msgr. Charles Joseph Morozzo (New York: Fr. Pustet & Co., 1901), 44. The translator's preface indicates that the original Latin text, *Cursus Vitae Spiritualis,* was originally published two and a quarter centuries earlier.

5. Sallie McFague, *The Body of God: An Ecological Theology* (Minneapolis: Fortress, 1993). McFague quotes this translation of chapter 1, "On God the Creator of All Things," as found in Grace Jantzen's *God's World, God's Body* (Philadelphia: Westminster Press, 1984). Jantzen's quotation is from *The Decrees of Vatican I,* ed. Vincent McNabb (London, 1907), 136.

6. McFague, *The Body of God,* 136. In her footnote she points to the important critiques of Vatican I's concept of God leveled by process theologians, including John Cobb and David Griffin (250).

7. Ibid., 192.

8. *Decrees of the First Vatican Council,* chapter 1, paragraph 11, *www.piar.hu/councils/ecum20.htm.*

Chapter 7: Fortitude

1. Nate Guidry, "Father Drowns Trying to Save Son," *Pittsburgh Post-Gazette,* May 30, 2006, A-1, A-6, and Jonathan D. Silver, "Boater Missing in 3rd Incident," *Pittsburgh Post-Gazette,* May 31, 2006, A-1, A-8.

2. *The Psalter* (Chicago: Liturgy Training Publications, 1995).

3. Winston Churchill, *The Second World War: Their Finest Hour,* vol. 2 (Boston: Houghton Mifflin, 1949), 115.

4. Ibid., 118.

5. This is the title of an article by Daniel Berrigan, S.J., in *Courage,* ed. Barbara Darling-Smith (Notre Dame, Ind.: University of Notre Dame Press, 2002).

6. Katherine Platt, "Guts Is a Habit: The Practice of Courage," in *Courage,* 134. In her footnote, Platt states that this model was influenced by the model of personal change of Wayne Jennings, presented to her along with other insights by Harriet Lansing.

Chapter 8: Communion

1. Joachim Wach, *The Comparative Study of Religions* (New York: Columbia, 1958). "The anthropologists, such as Marett and Malinowski, have proved that, far from being artificially induced ('invented,' as the age of enlightenment believed it to be), religion is an ubiquitous expression of the *sensus numinis* ['a sense of the presence of the holy'] (Otto's now famous term)," 38.

2. Ibid., 99–100.

3. Ibid., 114, 116.

4. Ibid., 127.

5. James White, *Introduction to Christian Worship* (Louisville: Westminster John Knox Press, 1992).

6. Lawrence S. Cunningham, *The Catholic Heritage* (New York: Crossroad, 1989), 134–35.

7. Joseph Martos, author of *Doors to the Sacred* (Liguori, Mo.: Liguori/Triumph, 2001), uses the image of "doors to the sacred" to describe the sacraments. "Window" is a useful variant.

8. Brian Doyle, "Celebrating Mass: Portland, Oregon," *Commonweal* 125, no. 2 (January 30, 1998): 19.

9. White, *Introduction to Christian Worship,* 126.

10. Kenan Osborne, O.F.M., *The Christian Sacraments of Initiation: Baptism, Confirmation and Eucharist* (New York: Paulist, 1987), 67, quoting the *Apostolic Tradition* of Hippolytus.

11. The specific theological character of the sacraments was articulated at the council. Joseph Martos summarizes its teachings that "not all of the sacraments were needed by each individual; that the sacraments did more than just nourish faith or publicly represent it; that some sacraments bestowed an indelible character on the soul with the result that they could be received only once; that all sacraments contained and conferred grace and so they were not just signs of grace that God was always offering to people; that God's grace was always offered through the sacraments even though individuals might place obstacles in the way of receiving that grace; that the grace of a sacrament was conferred by the rite itself and not by the faith of the recipient or the worthiness of the minister, that nevertheless performing the sacramental rites, ministers had to intend to do what the church did in order for them to be effective" (Martos, *Doors to the Sacred,* 91).

12. Words of Our Lady to Juan Diego, Our Lady of Guadalupe, *www.sancta.org.*

13. Shira Schoenberg, "The *Shema,*" *www.jewishvirtuallibrary.org.*

14. See the readable discussion of Jewish life and practices by Tracy R. Rich, "Judaism 101," *www.jewfaq.org.*

15. "How to Perform Salat," *www.submission.org.*

16. "A simple Buddhist altar, common to nearly all Buddhist traditions, has a Buddha statue or picture, and perhaps a candle, incense, and flowers. Ideally, Buddhist altars should be set [toward] the east; this is because the Buddha sat facing east beneath the

Bodhi Tree in Bodh Gaya, when he espied the morning star and experienced great enlightenment. The east is where the sun rises, illuminating us all. Of course, you can visualize this as being the case, regardless of where the altar is placed. A traditional Tibetan Buddhist altar has specific elements, placed on three levels. On the uppermost level is a central Buddha statue, and perhaps subsidiary statues. Other images, such as pictures and statues of lineage masters are arrayed on the second level or tier, along with symbolic elements such as a stupa (pagoda-shaped reliquary), holy relics, a dharma wheel, vital Buddhist texts, a mandala, a crystal, a conch shell, a censer, a bell or gong, and peacock feathers....In front of these, often on a lower third tier, are offerings to the things symbolized by the holy objects above. These offerings are represented by eight traditional silver or brass offering bowls, placed in a straight line, approximately one-eighth inch apart. They are filled with either water or the following separate offerings: water for drinking, water for washing, flowers, incense, light (candles or a lamp), perfume, food and music, and something representing clean clothes (a piece of silk, perhaps). These eight traditional offerings represent the things a devoted Buddhist householder in ancient India would offer the living Buddha and his monks and nuns when they came to visit. They are called the eight auspicious or significant offerings because they are associated with the arising Buddhist teachings in the world." See Lama Surya Das, "All About Altars," *www.beliefnet.com/story/86/story_8678.html.*

Conclusion

1. "On This Sad Day, 9-11," Editorial note, *www.submission.org.*

2. These reflections on the legitimacy of claims of religious truth are part of a paper on the religious experience of women survivors of domestic violence that I gave several years ago at a conference in Leuven, Belgium.

3. Haifa, Israel, Saturday, October 4, 2003: "At least 19 people were killed and 50 others injured when a female Palestinian suicide bomber set off an explosion yesterday in a landmark beachfront restaurant packed with a lunch crowd at the start of a long holiday

weekend....The Islamic Jihad militant group claimed responsibility for the attack in statements issued to television networks and wire services and identified the bomber as Hanadi Jaradat, a woman from Jenin who was in her twenties and had recently graduated from law school in Jordan. The statement said Jaradat had watched as Israeli troops shot and killed her brother and a cousin, both Islamic Jihad supporters, at their family home in June. Associates of Jaradat said that since the killing, she had become increasingly religious, reading from the Koran twice a day and fasting regularly." *Pittsburgh Post-Gazette,* October 5, 2003, A-1, A-4.

4. Stephen Bevans, *Models of Contextual Theology,* 7th ed. (Maryknoll, N.Y.: Orbis Books, 2002), 86, referring to David Tracy's argument from *Plurality and Ambiguity: Hermeneutics, Religion, Hope* (New York: Harper & Row, 1987), 18.

5. Bevans, *Models,* 86–87. Along with Tracy's argument, Bevans refers to Alyward Shorter's definition of "monoculturalism" in *Toward a Theology of Inculturation* (Maryknoll, N.Y.: Orbis Books, 1988), 18–20.

Of Related Interest

Paul Wadell
MORAL OF THE STORY
Learning from Literature about Human and Divine Love

According to Paul Wadell, great theology can be found in great literature. Wadell invites his readers to step into the fascinating worlds of five great texts. Walker Percy's *The Second Coming* highlights the call to choose life over death each day. Graham Greene's *The Heart of the Matter* probes the mysteries of human waywardness and God's inexhaustible love. Mary Gordon's *Final Payments* asks whether we can love everyone in the same way. Athol Fugard's play *My Children! My Africa!* delves into how injustice can be overcome. And Anne Tyler's novel *Saint Maybe* draws us into the question of forgiving and being forgiven.

Students of literature and professors of religion alike will be drawn into the compelling moral universe of these great works and see anew the power of great storytelling to transform life.

Each chapter includes a list of suggested readings for further exploration of these timeless themes.

Paul J. Wadell (Ph.D., University of Notre Dame) is Associate Professor of Religious Studies at St. Norbert College, De Pere, Wisconsin. He is the author of *Friendship and the Moral Life, The Primacy of Love: An Introduction to the Ethics of Thomas Aquinas,* and *Becoming Friends: Worship, Justice, and the Practices of Christian Friendship.*

ISBN 0-8245-1980-9, paper

crossroad

Of Related Interest

Francis R. Smith
THE WORLD IS CHARGED
The Transcendent with Us

*Includes study guide – the standard text for courses
in Catholic fundamental theology*

This book addresses a pressing need in classrooms everywhere to explain the unique nature of the Christian God. Fr. Smith observes that many intelligent and well-educated Catholics understand transcendence in a way that denies Jesus' humanity. By clarifying the divinity and transcendence of Jesus, Smith has been able to remove a number of misconceptions about Christology and help students grasp other fundamental theological issues more clearly as well. *The World Is Charged* is an important addition to college and seminary reading lists.

Francis R. Smith, S.J., is an experienced teacher and writer on major themes in Catholic theology. A native Californian, he earned his BS degree at Santa Clara University, in Santa Clara, California, completed his doctorate at the Gregorian University, and returned to Santa Clara University, where for decades he has served as a respected teacher, colleague, and rector of the Jesuit community. He is author of *The God Question: A Catholic Approach.*

ISBN 0-8245-2116-1, paper

crossroad

Of Related Interest

Ronald Rolheiser
AGAINST AN INFINITE HORIZON
The Finger of God in Our Everyday Lives

Full of personal anecdotes, healing wisdom, and a fresh reflection on Scripture, *Against an Infinite Horizon* draws on the great traditions of parable and storytelling. In this prequel to the bestselling *Holy Longing,* Rolheiser's new fans will be delighted with further insights into community, social justice, sexuality, mortality, and the deep beauty and poetry of Christian spirituality.

0-8245-1965-5, paper

Check your local bookstore for availability.
To order directly from the publisher,
please call 1-800-707-0670 for Customer Service
or visit our Web site at *www.cpcbooks.com.*
For catalog orders, please send your request to the address below.

THE CROSSROAD PUBLISHING COMPANY
16 Penn Plaza, Suite 1550
New York, NY 10001

All prices subject to change.

crossroad